P9-ASN-117

FIRESIDE

ALEX COMFORT

A GOOD AGE

Illustrated by Michael Leonard
(Including the mezzotints in
the Introduction)

A FIRESIDE BOOK
PUBLISHED BY SIMON AND SCHUSTER

Copyright © 1976 by Mitchell Beazley Publishers Limited
All rights reserved
including the right of reproduction
in whole or in part in any form
A Fireside Book
Published by Simon and Schuster
A Division of Gulf & Western Corporation
Simon & Schuster Building
Rockefeller Center
1230 Avenue of the Americas
New York, New York 10020

Manufactured in the United States of America

1   2   3   4   5   6   7   8   9   10

Library of Congress Cataloging in Publication Data

Comfort, Alexander, 1920-
    A good age.

    (A Fireside book)
    Bibliography: p.
    Includes index.
    1. Aged. 2. Aging. I. Title.
QP86.C58   1978   612.6'7   77-18925
ISBN 0-671-24233-4

    1. Aged.   2. Aging.   I. Title.

For my father on his ninety-third birthday

Contents

Introduction

FALSTAFF: You that are old consider not the capacities
of us that are young; you measure the heat of our livers
with the bitterness of your galls; and we that are in the
vanguard of youth, I must confess, are wags too.

THE LORD CHIEF JUSTICE: Do you set down your name in the
scroll of youth, that are written down old with all the
characters of age? Have you not a moist eye, a dry hand,
a yellow cheek, a white beard, a decreasing leg, an
increasing belly? Is not your voice broken, your wind short,
your chin double, your wit single, and every part about you
blasted with antiquity, and will you yet call yourself young?
Fie, fie, fie, Sir John!

FALSTAFF: My Lord, I was born about three of the clock,
in the afternoon, with a white head, and something a round
belly. For my voice, I have lost it with hollaing, and singing
of anthems. To approve my youth further, I will not: the truth is,
I am only old in judgment and understanding; and he that
will caper with me for a thousand marks, let him lend me the
money, and have at him!

William Shakespeare, *Henry IV*, part 2; Act 1, Scene 2

There are two kinds of aging. One is biological, and expresses itself in such changes as the graying of hair, the decline in eye-focusing power and the loss of top-register hearing. The most serious of these changes is the increased liability to, and lack of recuperative power from, illnesses of various kinds, which shows itself as the rising "force of mortality," and makes a man seventy-five years old about forty-one times more likely to die during that year of his life than a man of twenty. The mechanism of this loss of vigor is not yet fully understood, but it is under investigation and the rate of loss, like any other biological rate, can almost certainly be artificially slowed. Science is on the verge of attempting this slowing in humans. The science devoted to it is experimental gerontology, which is likely to be the area of some of the greatest advances in medicine by the year 2000.

How we fare individually with this sort of aging depends upon three factors—luck, money and genetic inheritance. There may soon be an active way of attacking it; at the moment there is not. But the things which make oldness insupportable in human societies don't at all commonly arise from consequences of this biological aging process. They arise from "sociogenic aging." This means, quite simply, the role which society imposes on people as they reach a certain chronologic age. At this age they "retire" or, in plain words, are rendered unemployed, useless and, in some

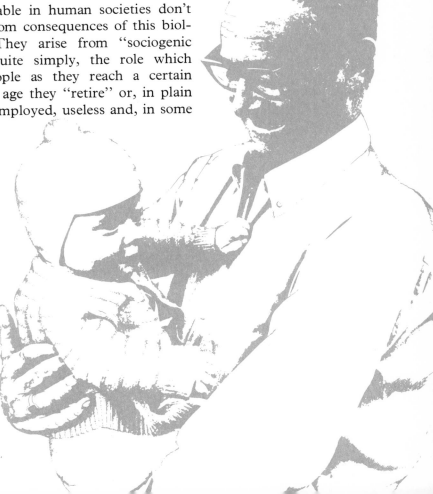

cases, impoverished. After that transition, and in proportion to their chronological age, they are prescribed to be unintelligent, unemployable, crazy and asexual.

Prescription is a nasty and familiar process. It commonly involves two principles—the unpeople principle and the expendable people principle. We have become so used to the application of these principles to "the old"—the people who differ from others in the length of time they have lived—that it's easier to recognize them in other unlovable applications. Remember when black people were "different," unemployable in many jobs and expendable unpeople? Remember when women had defined roles, but were too emotional to undertake this, that and the other (and when, in both instances, the victims were supposed to recognize their imaginary limitations and like them)? The trouble with this kind of black magic directed at a group is that if the words are said often enough, the victims half believe it themselves, until something happens to expose the lie.

Lies about aging are especially hard to expose. When society penalized blacks, or Jews, or women, the victims lived with prejudice all their lives—and some of them had had time to debrainwash themselves and to fight back, building a basis of civil rights on which others could stand. The trouble is that we aren't born old. Society's prejudices indoctrinate us before they hit us. (How many twenty-year-olds realize that sexual capacity and normal intelligence are lifelong in healthy

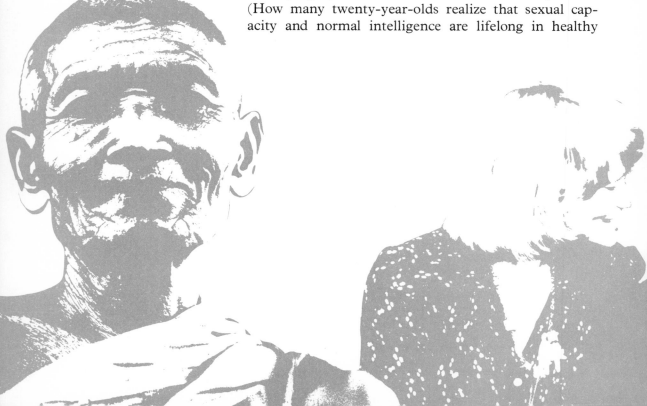

humans?) On this basis we obligingly drown ourselves as persons when the clock points to the appropriate age.

Modern research indicates that a high proportion of the mental and attitudinal changes seen in "old" people are not biological effects of aging. They are the results of role playing. When women were expected to faint at the sight of blood, or black people to be amiable Uncle Toms, some of them did and were; now that those roles are seen to be demeaning or ridiculous, they don't and aren't. Role playing is natural and useful in some contexts. It's difficult to be a doctor or a general or a hard hat without to some extent playing the part. The trouble with the part we assign to "the old," is that it is a destructive part. They are supposed to be physically and intellectually infirm, slow on the uptake and rigid in their ways. We've had justified protests at children's books which show boys as active and girls as passive, because this insidious training falsifies sex roles. Consider how "old age" has been depicted, and you will see why so many people get to the stage where they would rather avoid taking aptitude and skill tests than risk doing them and being found senile.

Research on physical aging is a necessity, because it is the only way in which we can generate protection against, or postponement of, real physical problems like arthritis and brain disease. It has been held up for years because the culture regarded aging as natural and, in contrast with older peasant societies, set out to exagger-

ate it by demeaning and excluding the old. Victorian doctors' offices were filled not with degenerative diseases like high blood pressure and cancer, but with infectious diseases. It was "natural," edifying and probably the will of God that every family should lose several children from such diseases as scarlatina, diphtheria and typhoid. Sermons were preached about it (as they have been about the naturalness of aging). In 1861, in London, Queen Victoria's immensely popular husband, Prince Albert, died of typhoid, with the assistance of six physicians. This was at the close of the Great Exhibition of technology, which he had organized, and *The Times* christened medicine "the withered arm of science." At some point, it seems, society throughout Europe decided that enough was enough. Within twenty years it had Koch, Ehrlich, Lister, Pasteur and the beginnings of the rout of infectious diseases.

Science has not so far made a concentrated attack on the degenerative diseases, partly because it does not yet have the knowledge, and partly because it lacks the will. That is changing. In de Tocqueville's words "the evil which was suffered patiently as inevitable seems unendurable as soon as the idea of escaping from it crosses men's minds." That is happening now. Most of us are going to die of age-dependent diseases. These can only be picked off singly to a limited extent, and the best chance of improving our mileage lies in a medicine of rate control.

While that is developing, the things we individually can do to improve our own aging, and that of others, lie overwhelmingly in the sociogenic sector. The most important of these is the militant exposure of society's stupid callousness to those who reach a given year, and of the hogwash by which that callousness is maintained. This change of mind is also needed if medicine is to advance. Research requires funds, and the convention that the old are "different" from ourselves—and so can be ignored, as whites ignored blacks and men put down women—prevents us from acting in our own behalf. By ignoring an oppressed minority which we are inevitably going to join, we do not realize that we are slashing our own tires.

The salient fact is obvious enough. "Old" people are people who have lived a certain number of years, and *that is all*. If they have physical problems, so do younger people. I recall a panel on which there served a brilliant woman doctor in her eighties who was deaf and, for that reason, had difficulty joining in the discussion. It was instructive to see how she was passed over as a non-contributor by people who would have taken trouble to ensure that a deaf woman of twenty was fully included.

Unless we are old already, the next "old people" will be us. Whether we go along with the kind of treatment meted out to those who are now old depends upon how far society can sell us the bill of goods it sold them—and it depends more upon that than upon any research. No

pill or regime known, or likely, could transform the latter years of life as fully as could a change in our vision of age and a militancy in attaining that change.

Bad as our unpeopling of "old" people is when the age of happy dispatch is sixty-five, society has not finished yet. The United Auto Workers, for example, already retires people at fifty-five, if they promise to quit the industry. Quite recently a report to a Senate sub-committee indicated that twenty years would be the economic life of most blue-collar workers twenty-five years later so that employment could be maintained in the face of increasing mechanization. In other words, they would be retiring, and, if we go on as we are, dumped from society, at the age of thirty-nine. Forty-year retirement contracts are things of the past. Thirty-year contracts are on the way out—roll on the twenty-year contracts! As this happens, if we let it happen, one of two things will occur. Either we reprogram society to find new engagement for the people it dumps or we declare them unpeople and discover a stack of bogus-science grounds for believing that ineptitude, nonhumanness, dependency, unintelligence and lack of dignity start at the age of thirty-nine.

Education, similarly, is based on unpeople folklore. People aren't educated to live, however much mouthing is done by the education industry. They are educated to act as work-oriented kamikazes, one-way projectiles. Accordingly, they get from twelve to twenty years of educational training, after which they are, as it were, fired. There is no need to give them any but purely technological updating, because at the end of their trajectory they are designed to explode—no deposit, no return. With fewer children, earlier job ejection and more educated and highly expecting citizens, this program is on its last legs. The education of the future, besides being lifelong, will have to be designed to further a second trajectory, not a one-shot mission, so as to generate lifetime pilots, not kamikazes. Having to stop work as an assembly-line operator is not necessarily a tragedy. If society chooses, and we insist, it can also be an opportunity (to get an education one didn't get, for example, if one so chooses)—provided, however, that we do not insist that the retired person doesn't need to eat, or at least doesn't need to eat much.

In America sheer poverty is not the leading curse of oldness. It is one curse, because people who have always been poor stay so when they are old, with all the attendant subcurses of bad health, bad housing, low self-esteem and exploitation which descend on poor people. Nevertheless, the percentage of poor over the age of sixty-five has gone down dramatically, from 29·6 in 1967 to 18·6 in 1972. Social Security payments alone have gone up by 70 percent in five years, although this does not allow for inflation, which has hit both savings and fixed-level interest and pensions. (Some of the worst distress recently was in Florida. There people who were

well off when they retired are now living on welfare.)

The real curse of being old is the ejection from a citizenship traditionally based on work. In other words, it is a demeaning idleness, nonuse, not being called on any longer to contribute, and hence being put down as a spent person of no public account, instructed to run away and play until death comes out to call us to bed. This is something the Supplemental Security Incomes plan can't deal with. There is in fact marginally more chance of useful social involvement for an old person in a ghetto than for a retired executive pitched into a life of uninterrupted golf or reading paperbacks, who may not recognize that he has been sold a second, noncivic childhood along with the condominium key.

Nobody demands that every man and woman have unlimited tenure. Some people do become incapable with the passage of time; others always were incapable. But others only became "incapable" because they imagine themselves to be so, and society reinforces that imagining. At the age of sixty-eight, Thomas Jefferson wrote to Benjamin Rush: "I have resumed the study (of mathematics) with great avidity. I have forgotten much, and recover it with more difficulty than when in the vigor of my mind I originally acquired it. It is wonderful to me that old men should not be sensible that their minds keep pace with their bodies in the progress of decay. Our old revolutionary friend Clinton, who was a hero but never a man of the mind, is wonderfully jealous on

that head. He tells eternally the stories of his younger days to prove his memory, as if memory and reason were the same faculty. Nothing betrays imbecility so much as being insensible of it. Had not a conviction of the danger to which an unlimited occupation of the executive chair would expose the republican constitution of government made it conscientiously a duty to retire when I did, the fear of becoming a dotard and of being insensible to it would of itself have resisted all solicitations to remain."

For tradition to have mesmerized the sixty-eight-year-old Jefferson, who was ailing, into a conviction of his own imbecility is no mean feat. While Clinton, who was never very bright, anxiously tested his memory and bored everyone around him, Jefferson assumed that he was losing the grip which he actually retained for another fifteen years. A better reason for retiring occurs in the same letter: "There is a fullness of time when men should go, and not occupy too long the ground to which others have a right to advance."

In bees, a change in social role is programmed with the passage of time. There is no reason why it should not be so in people. We move, after all, from being children to being parents and then to being grandparents. What is unique in our culture is that older people are made arbitrarily roleless. Some avoid this, because people are more sensible than society, but it is the accepted pattern. Other cultures weight the social position of people with time by giving status to seniority. This is biologically

sensible because some skills, such as physical endurance, do indeed decline with age, but normal people more than make up for this by using experience to cut their effort. What has hit our culture is a combination of factors unusual for man. One, which may be expected to increase in effect, is the decline of the family, both as a social force and in numbers, leading to a shortage of kin. The kinship role of being a grandparent, across the large distances created by American mobility, comes second to an independence which cherishes lack of family commitment, and expects the old to be "independent." This is not a bad objective, nor can the process now be run backward, but it has created casualties.

Another factor is the rate-of-change effect. Although an old attorney is an experienced attorney, even something as elephantine as the law now changes fast. An "old" electronics man, meaning one who stops updating, will be obsolete in a couple of years. No experience, even of living, now counts for credit. Yet another factor is an advertising-fed youth cult. The TV ratings stop at forty-nine, for people over that age, say the advertisers, have "brand loyalty" formed, are too experienced to be ripped off and have no money anyway.

The answer does not of course lie in life tenure for everyone. The United States wisely limits the tenure of presidents (although not by age) and if ineducable people didn't die or get eased out nothing would change. Agism is used, however, as a substitute for control. The judge who is eased out by retirement is said to be senile, as the vagaries of the late J. Edgar Hoover were excused by age, when the fact is usually that the retiring age is treated as a welcome kybosh on someone who was always unfit for his office. The answer to the can-of-worms complexity of promotion, unemployment and career structure doesn't lie in patriarchal tenure (enemies of retirement are often professors who will never "retire" so long as they can talk or write, rarely longshoremen), but rather in lifelong education and serial careers. Lifelong education is likely to be favored by the shortage-of-kin effect resulting from zero population growth. In the next few years, education will be a dying industry unless it shifts to the higher age groups. Serial careers don't involve reappointing the president of the company as janitor, but in recognizing the continued growth and achievement of people, and giving them, at a set age, the option of retirement (which some will choose) and continued involvement in something quite new, with safeguards against their exploitation as cheap labor.

There are, of course, fields where experience still holds up. We all know of old violin makers, old actors and old orchestral conductors. Technology makes such built-in status rarer, however. To see it in its original form one needs to watch an old smith make a horseshoe in twelve strokes, using the skill of sixty-odd years to substitute for brute force. In much machinery-based work, this no longer applies, although it could do so, now that goods

are moved with forklifts, not humped around on shoulders. The argument for a clean break is not based on make-work, but on the recognition it implies of continued growth and the continued ability to learn, for those who want it that way.

One wholly negative way of dealing with age, which is natural enough in view of the low esteem attached to being old, but which also comes under the heading of rip-offs, because it is actively promoted, is to deny it—with wigs, cosmetics, silicones and Pollyannaish attitudes. Women are more prone to this than men because of the basic injustice which decrees that by tradition men of any age are sexually competitive while older women aren't. At the same time, one can only beat this by not going along with it.

This book is not about denial. There is tragedy in the physical transformation of the human body, and the mind has to live with this transformation, although it is unchanged itself except for the social and apparent changes in its vehicle. This aspect of aging is like an involuntary change of dress. This is the way Proust described his return to a house he knew after a lapse of years: "At first I could not understand why I found some difficulty in recognizing the master of the house and the guests, and why everyone there was made up—a makeup that usually included powder and altered them entirely. The prince had provided himself with a white beard and, as it were, lead soles which dragged at his feet. A name

was mentioned to me, and I was dumbfounded at the thought that it applied to the blonde waltzing girl I had once known and to the stout white-haired lady now walking just in front of me. We did not see our own appearance, our own age, but each, like a facing mirror, saw the other's."

The wearers of the makeup may or may not feel "old," however—few people who are not sick or depressed do—but in our culture they may find themselves alone in realizing that there is a young person, the same person, inside. Older people are in fact young people inhabiting old bodies and confronted with the physical problems of reduced vigor, changing appearance and, although many escape these, specific disabilities affecting such things as sight and agility.

It will help when science can suppress or slow the physical changes, and this would, to some extent, overcome the incomprehension of the younger person for the old. This is the kind of technical fix on which we over-rely, and if we rely on it exclusively there is something a little unworthy about it. It is rather as if we say that we could end race prejudice if we could turn all black people white.

The attacks on aging now being marshaled aim to slow it down, not to stop it altogether, and their outcome at best will be to make it take, say, seventy years to reach today's physical sixty. The peculiar situation of sociogenic "age" makes concerned and self-concerned

common sense about it difficult to acquire. This is because it hits us unprepared on a fixed date and, until we have to think about it, we avoid the idea of it ("probably won't live that long") or panic in middle age when we see it approaching. When societies mistreat a group they usually do so through fear.

Change is inevitable in the assessment of aging and in the treatment of the aged. For a start, more and more people today survive to the age at which we now set "oldness," and, consequently, some 20 percent or more of the population of the United States will be sixty-five or over by the year 2000. Moreover, regardless of their prosperity, or lack of it, in earlier years, those who will then be sixty-five will, on the average, have higher expectations—financial, sexual, social and self-regarding—than "the old" of today. How they will act in their own defense is not yet clear. In the past "the old" have not been a very effective lobby and have tended to be exploited politically by fringe movements. The line this growing constituency will take in the future is anyone's guess. The major parties may compete for its favor, or it may develop its own lobby.

The role of the media, which at present cater little to seniors because their financing objectives do not include them, will probably grow. Twenty percent of the public will be more than 20 percent of the steady audience of the media because one physical effect of age is decline in mobility and, therefore, greater dependence upon radio, television and the press. There is a means here of catering to needs, of giving information and of stereotype busting, which will need a sharp effort like that which got black figures more dignified and realistic treatment in entertainment. Short of this, the scripts will go on falsifying age along the old lines.

To change things in a democracy one has ultimately to lie down on the tracks and say, "Stop." The new old will be more willing, I think, to do this than are the now old; when the now old were young, even in the stormy early days of labor unions, protest was less an organ of orderly political change than it is today. This book is not only for the now old. All people, of all ages, need the basic facts to contrast with the stereotype. Those now old need survival strategies. Those who are not yet called old need to realize what is in store for them if they let things ride. That is what this book is about.

A well-meaning young Senator was showing a party of seniors around the Senate Chamber. He treated them a little like schoolchildren; explaining the legislative process in words of one syllable and shouting in case they were deaf. Finally, turning to one of the group, the Senator asked, "And what used you to be?" The old man fixed a beady eye on him and replied, "I still am."

Let us look at the stereotype of the ideal aged American as past folklore presents it. He or she is a white-haired, inactive, unemployed person, making no demands on

anyone, least of all the family, docile in putting up with loneliness, rip-offs of every kind and boredom, and able to live on a pittance. He or she, although not demented, which would be a nuisance to other people, is slightly deficient in intellect and tiresome to talk to, because folklore says that old people are weak in the head, asexual, because old people are incapable of sexual activity, and it is unseemly if they are not. He or she is unemployable, because old age is second childhood and everyone knows that the old make a mess of simple work. Some credit points can be gained by visiting or by being nice to a few of these subhuman individuals, but most of them prefer their own company and the company of other aged unfortunates. Their main occupations are religion, grumbling, reminiscing and attending the funerals of friends. If sick, they need not, and should not, be actively treated, and are best stored in unsupervised institutions run by racketeers who fleece them and hasten their demise. A few, who are amusing or active, are kept by society as pets. The rest are displaying unpardonable bad manners by continuing to live, and even on occasion by complaining of their treatment, when society has declared them unpeople and their patriotic duty is to lie down and die.

If this picture of aging offends you, visit a few of the places where old people are kept. If you dislike what you see, recognize that you have a few years to change it before the stereotype hits you. If it has hit you already,

you will know it better than anyone and you will want any help available to fight back.

The odd thing about this unlovely stereotype, apart from the fact that it is wholly untrue, is that it is relatively recent. Throughout history and in most cultures the old person is a figure of recourse. There is the fisherman, now retired from fishing, whom the village nevertheless consults if the fishing goes sour, because he is the only one who saw this happen before. There is the woman who has ten children and has delivered hundreds, who knows what to do with a difficult labor. Any infirmity such people have is considered a misfortune to the community, because it limits their contribution.

In not-so-distant America, even in pioneering towns where youth for obvious reasons predominated, the old-timer was the bearded figure, less agile than he had been, who was still a crack shot, or the apple-faced lady who in an emergency could drive a team like a devil out of hell. These were romanticized stereotypes and they were false, too. Every age has those to whom aging brings some degree of personal crumbling and disaster, but at least the romantic stereotype neither demeans persons of long life nor lays on them our own fears and false imaginings. In peasant societies there is no ejection; the old man or woman who no longer plows or reaps (as many do into the eighties), still feeds the chickens or hulls the peas, and decline if it must occur is gentler and not a summary ejection into a kind of tacit contempt.

There are in fact encouraging signs that the obnoxious stereotype of age, at least in its blackest form, is already out of date. In a study conducted in 1975 for the National Council on Aging by the Louis Harris Company, 74 percent of the public saw "the old" as friendly and warm, 64 percent as wise from experience, 41 percent as physically active, 35 percent as effectual and proficient, 29 percent as alert, but only 21 percent as adaptable and only 5 percent as sexually active. This implies a substantial shift from myth to reality. Unfortunately, many public attitudes are still predicated on the myth. Significantly, while 82 percent of people between eighteen and sixty-four reckoned sixty-five-and-over seniors to be friendly, only 25 percent over sixty-five thought their fellow seniors to be so. Five percent of the young thought of the old as "very sexually active," 6 percent of the old thought so of old people generally and 11 percent were so themselves. In fact, although the poll showed a surprising proportion of American seniors to be both socially and economically contented and happy with the latter years of their lives, there is a hint that others have been imprinted with the negative attitude to themselves and to their age which fear of aging generates.

All in all, then, the public's image of oldsters is generally much more negative than that which oldsters have of themselves as people, not as members of a group. They consider themselves open-minded, bright, active, adaptable and sexually active, but "old folks" generally are not—"I'm fine, but then, I'm an exception." Individuals have as much confidence in themselves as do the young; it's the others who follow the stereotype. Along the same line, one in three people over sixty-five finds his or her present life better than he or she had expected it would be; while only one in ten finds it worse, and then often because of unanticipated boredom, sickness or bereavement.

There are two put-down and alarming views of aging in America. One is generated by thoughtless agism and the other by overstating the injustices inflicted on the old in order to reform them. This book subscribes to neither view. Old age in America, except for those to whom society has never given their due share as human beings, is more prosperous than in many, and perhaps most, other countries. On the other hand, there are countries where the standard of living of the old is far lower, but where their involvement in society and their sense of worth are greater. The changes which could remedy this deficit and evoke the full intellectual and physical powers which human beings possess lifelong, are changes of attitude. Once an older person comes to be seen, not as old first and provisionally a person second, but as a person who happens also to be old, and who is still as he or she always was, plus experience and minus the consequences of certain physical accidents of time—only then will social gerontology have made its point.

This book is not a handbook of social services, where to get insurance or diet recipes. It is basically about attitudes to aging, your own attitude and that of others. If we go on about organization and protest, that is because aging as you will experience it is not a biological or a physical transformation. It is a political transformation which is laid upon you after a set number of years, and the ways of dealing with it are political and attitudinal.

The attitudinal lessons are simple and worth comparing with what you already believe or feel about "aging."

1. Aging has no effect upon you as a person. When you are "old" you will feel no different and be no different from what you are now or were when you were young, except that more experiences will have happened. In age your appearance will change, however, and you may encounter more physical problems. When you do, these will affect you only as physical problems affect a person of any age. An "aged" person is simply a person who has been there longer than a young person.

2. "Oldness" is a political institution and a social convention, based on a system which expels people from useful work after a set number of years. This institution is bolstered by a large body of ignorant folklore which justifies the expulsion by depicting those expelled as weak-minded, incompetent and increasingly fatuous. None of this folklore is true.

3. Retirement is another name for dismissal and unemployment. It must be prepared for exactly as you would prepare for dismissal and unemployment.

4. You are about to join an underprivileged minority. There is no way of avoiding this at present. The remedies available to you will be those available to other minorities—organization, protest and militancy. Don't get trapped into aging alone if you can help it. The time to organize and get into a posture to resist is before the floor falls out.

5. At a set age you will be deprived of half your income. There are some benefits you can and should demand by right, but these won't compensate. You will be poorer than you think at a time when you need more than now, so prepare and reinsure if you can. Best of all, stay in paid useful work.

6. On the other hand, you need not count on illness or decrepitude. Your memory, sexuality, activity, capacity for relationships and zest should normally last as long as you do, and do last in the majority of people. When they do not, it is for the same cause as in earlier years, namely illness.

7. Science is nearer than most people realize to attempting the slowing of the health deterioration of age so that vigor lasts longer and death comes later. It is not likely either to abolish age changes or to reverse

them in the foreseeable future. How fast it progresses in slowing them depends almost wholly upon social investment.

8. You are "created" old by society in the same way that an English worthy is "created" a Lord, but this honor is negative. Those who have had it conferred on them, however, will total up to 20 percent of the population of America by 2000, enough to raise a ruckus if they get together and ensure they are not, as now, picked off singly. When this happens, either the title will stop being conferred or it will change significantly in meaning.

9. As an "old" person, you will need four things— dignity, money, proper medical services and useful work. They are exactly the things you always needed. As things are today, you won't get them, but there is no divinely ordered reason why you should not. So, either set out now to see that you do get them or work to force society to change its posture—or do both.

Remember that aging is not a radical change. You will not become a different person. Your physical and social needs will not alter, your sources of value will not change. But you will have been assiduously trained by past indoctrination to think that aging is a change in yourself. Except for limited physical alterations it isn't. It is much more like a peculiarly shaped social hat which you are required to put on so that you may become

identified as a statutory unperson. It is a hat which can't be refused, in present circumstances, but it can be taken off and jumped on if you don't like the look of it.

Getting these attitudes over to people, "old" and not old, is probably the main outstanding task of social gerontology. Aging as a physical change is relatively unimportant compared with aging as a social nonevent. The only necessary losses of age (necessary because some of them occur to everyone) are physical. All the other losses which we see as the natural consequences of being over sixty, over seventy or over eighty are unnecessary, organizational, conventional.

Physical losses are serious and will ultimately kill us. At the same time, only the most fortunate have lived up to old age without some losses of this kind, either gradual (most of us would not still wish to play football at forty) or catastrophic (like a broken leg which leaves us with a limp). Up to "old age," and even with major disablement, most people simply, in Beethoven's words, take life by the throat. This is a lot more difficult when neighbors and friends stand around saying, "Ah well, can't expect too much, he's getting on," or "She's not as young as she was," or worse have implied that there is something rather fitting in losing faculties and going downhill simply because one has been around long enough.

Most older people do tackle disability with as much or more courage than at any other age. But this would be easier to do if there were not a "gate," on one side of

which deafness, for example, is a disability and the deaf person is helped to join in, while on the other side deafness is "natural" and the deaf person can be ignored or avoided as not worth talking with anyway. Aging as a physical problem is real and science has started to work on it. "Old age" as it is now sold is an imaginary state which need exist only as long as we believe it does and impose it on people by all kinds of economic and social pressures.

We can't take the pain out of the facts that humans aren't immortal or indefinitely disease-proof, or that illnesses accumulate as we age. We can, however, wholly abolish the mischievous idea that after a fixed age we become different, impaired or nonpeople. The start of

this demystification has to be in our own rejection of it for ourselves, and then in our refusal to impose it on others.

The entries in this book cover facts, self-defense measures, problems and also some of the plus factors and pleasures of later life. From the facts you can, whatever your age, debrainwash yourself about what is and isn't inherent in the passage of time. So long as society is what it is, self-defense is the main skill people need as they get older, and if we ignored the physical and social problems we could be creating a deception of our own. Bear in mind that while illnesses have to be included among these entries, you aren't about to have all, or necessarily any, of them. The remedies we suggest for old-age problems all carry the qualification "if you can afford them." This is a qualification imposed by the kind of society we live in. Pleasures need no comment. They can be real. Resources indicate where you can turn for help or organize it for yourself—and for others, which can be a resource and a pleasure in itself.

This book won't immediately alter society. On the other hand, there is nothing like the realization that "this needn't be so" to make men and women radical. The supposed conservatism and quietism of old people is a myth about to be exploded. They, as much as the young, can kick society in its social conscience.

Agism is the notion that people cease to be people, cease to be the same people or become people of a distinct and inferior kind, by virtue of having lived a specified number of years. The eighteenth-century French naturalist Georges Buffon said, "to the philosopher, old age must be considered a prejudice." Agism is that prejudice. Like racism, which it resembles, it is based on fear, folklore and the hang-ups of a few unlovable people who propagate these. Like racism, it needs to be met by information, contradiction and, when necessary, confrontation. And the people who are being victimized have to stand up for themselves in order to put it down.

Cecil B. De Mille, film producer-director and founding father of Hollywood, is famed principally for the large-scale epic productions of his later years. In 1952, when he was seventy-one, he produced and directed the Academy Award-winning *The Greatest Show on Earth*. His seventieth film, a new version of his first biblical movie, *The Ten Commandments*, had its premiere four years later.

Alcohol can get to be a major problem in old age for people who had no problems with it earlier. This is partly because tolerance for alcohol decreases, and partly because society may make age so stressful that people drink to escape it. The rules are the same, basically, as at any age—if you find you cannot do without alcohol you should drop it entirely, with professional help if need be. The average time it takes to convince an alcoholic that he or she has a medical problem is fifteen years, and in old age you don't have that long. Also, as at earlier ages, drinking is often a covert form of suicide.

You don't need to change stable drinking habits unless you find those habits are changing, or you had an unacknowledged drink problem all along. But remember that alcohol causes confusion and affects memory. It can also be fatally incompatible with many medications. You already run the risk of overmedication as you age. Alcohol impairs brain performance and increases the risk of falling—a major danger to the old. The older you are the more you need your head straight.

For people who are lonely, sick or have life problems, alcohol is a far more dangerous drug than heroin because it's around and all your well-meaning friends are pushers. If it gets beyond wine or beer occasionally with meals or one glass of any other liquor per day, you're probably giving hostages to fortune.

Alcoholism can be dealt with at any age, but you need expert help—call your local chapter of Alcoholics Anonymous or one of the other organizations listed in the phone book. In old age few things break up a person faster than alcoholism.

Arthritis means inflammatory damage to a joint. Along with other kinds of pain when you move, it is often wrongly called rheumatism. Rheumatoid arthritis is a crippling disease of relatively young adults. The arthritis characteristic of age is correctly called "degenerative joint disease." It occurs in the fingers, knees, hips and vertebrae in that order of frequency. It is usually not crippling, although it can make movement painful and stiff. It is worse with exercise and is relieved by rest; it commonly follows damage or overuse of joints affected through past occupation. One kind of overuse of weight-bearing joints is obesity—you have been carrying more weight than the joint bearings will stand. Gout is a separate disease with different treatment (and is not confined to claret-drinking Regency aldermen—it occurs in teetotalers and women).

Bad arthritis in age can be disabling; minor arthritis is a painful, limiting nuisance. It is a disease, not a natural hardship of chronologic age, and it can be treated. The sheet anchor of this treatment is common aspirin, but don't treat every minor joint pain yourself. From the age of fifty onward, go to your doctor regularly for any persistent pain or stiffness so that incipient arthritis can be treated. Besides aspirin, treatment can include hormones, gold injections and such accessory programs as weight loss. Ideally, you would avoid punishing your joints earlier in life by such occupational hazards as power tools which vibrate, but even if you have neglected this kind of preventive medicine, early checkups can halt arthritic damage before it gets disabling.

If it has already got disabling, strategy consists of active medical treatment combined with life planning to circumvent any limitation of movement which you may have—shorter hair if you can't reach to comb it, housing which doesn't involve difficult stairs. It is not "normal" for seniors to be "arthritic," or won't be when they get proper preventive treatment from middle life, and even if arthritic changes develop they can be held at bay—but only by proper, active attention from a competent physician or clinic.

In the final crunch, useless painful joints can be fused by surgery (giving you a fixed knee or elbow which is, however, painless and useful) or actually replaced with an artificial joint. This kind of repair can turn you from a housebound cripple into a fully active person, with all the psychological gains which that implies. It is one of the instances when an artificial prosthesis is life-changing. But the key to prevention here is probably early checkup and early assessment of any persistent pain or stiffness—probably, because no generation has yet had this kind of presenior maintenance.

The danger of aspirin is that it is so effective, and underlying mischief may not be recognized if it is painless or if you can stop the pain by self-medication. There are other resources for stiffness, from hot pads to liniment. Use these by all means, but don't assume that the fact you keep needing them more and more often is an expected concomitant of aging, like gray hair. If your joints often hurt there is something wrong with

❛For as I like a young man in whom there is something of the old, so I like an old man in whom there is something of the young; and he who follows this maxim, in body will possibly be an old man, but he will never be an old man in mind.❜

Cicero

37

them. The condition will get worse and may disable you unless you check it out, as you would have done at thirty or forty. There shouldn't be any pain requiring heating pads, aspirin or liniment beyond the occasional strain or stiffness which we all get from sitting in a draft. Anything more calls for medical inquiries and proper tests. Your mobility is the next most important asset after your wits, so be aggressive in guarding it. Far more money is spent annually in promoting quack and palliative commercial remedies than is allocated in the entire U.S. budget for preventive and curative arthritis medicine.

Bereavement. Ernest Hemingway wrote that "there is no happy ending to a genuine love affair." At the same time an ending is inevitable, in view of human mortality. In a sense, bereavement in later life is "no different" from bereavement when we are younger, and could be less of a bombshell because it is expected, or at least seen as a contingency to be thought about. On the other hand, late in life most couples resemble two beams propped against each other, and if one is pulled out a whole life pattern, which was in viable equilibrium, collapses.

There is no way of *dealing* with bereavement so as to make it painless. Neither the British technique of pretending death didn't happen nor the American mortician-promoted technique of cosmetics, rip-offs and open caskets work. Both tend only to limit the overt expression of normal emotions of grief, rage and despair, which then surface a bit later as depression or illness. Bereaved people tend to be quite unexpectedly boycotted by friends who don't know how to handle death—and stay away.

Bereavement, when it comes, can only be lived through. On the other hand, it can be prepared for, and not only when a lifetime partner becomes ill in a threatening way. Thinking through each other's possible deaths at least once—economically, practically, emotionally—isn't ghoulish or bad luck. It is loving, because each partner is considering the preservation of the other. There is nothing loving in asserting that if X dies you will die of grief. You won't, and you do X no honor by promising to live in a state of misery.

You normally take out insurance for a surviving partner. Take out survivor insurance by having a

38

mutually agreed plan of reaction which will go into operation automatically if death should occur. First you need to allow time—eight weeks is average—for mourning, confusion and the state of being "shut down." In planning from then on, remember that all relict spouses at all ages are more vulnerable in health for a year after bereavement. Set up a program which can take over from your own willpower until it recovers. Arrange machinery so that financial business and other transactions operate without you or operate automatically during the mourning period, but not so that you can't immerse yourself in them if you find that helpful.

Having a schedule like that of the astronauts' space re-entry, which removes the need to improvise, is the best insurance against the shock, emptiness and strangeness which follow loss. Long-term improvisations can come later, in response to circumstances then obtaining, but the time for your fire drill is early in life, with regular updates on all arrangements. You may feel queasy the first time, but remember that fire drills don't cause fires.

Often the unspoken aspects of bereavement do the most damage. One of these is relief. *All* long-term partners, however loving, have a perfectly comprehensible sense of relief mingled with desolation at losing a companion, and many react to this component (which is especially strong when there has been a long, trying illness), not by recognition, but by guilt at their lack of proper emotion and by idealizing the dead person. This is a major contributor to "widower's impotency" at re-marriage (see *Sex*).

People vary in their handling of actual grief. Some are helped by keeping everything as it was, as if the dead person were on holiday, others by turning out every vestige of the lost person and rearranging the house. Don't be guilty about this strategy either, if you select it. You are not destroying their memory, only asserting that you must now embark on a new life trajectory.

Rehearsal by discussion, when you are both present and well, may limit some of the strong, irrational re-actions you will have in the event. Financial as well as emotional rehearsal is essential (so you know where all the keys, papers, etc., are). You may like to carry out this exercise with help (from an attorney or from a counselor). Oddly enough, you will not find it depressing in fact, although it sounds a downer in prospect. Women in particular, who, because of longer life and the fact they are often younger than their husbands, face a high chance of being widows, are often deeply relieved once it has been done.

The point of having expert help is that deep and unfaced emotions are involved. Handled properly a death rehearsal can open up a marriage, but you don't want to do this with a crowbar or you may have trouble getting it back together. One recalls the French king whose wife on her deathbed told him lovingly that he must remarry. "No! No!" blubbered the king, "I'd rather have mistresses!" Spouses have to be able, ideally, to accept the idea that "their" person can and will if necessary go on without them, and even find new resources in the experience. They need also to accept that they themselves can and will if necessary go on without their partner and find new resources there, too, which does not preclude grief at loss, gratitude for what has been and loyalty to a relationship now discharged to the full. If these things are indeed faced, and the relationship is deepened by facing them, bereavement is not painless. Grief will and should be felt and expressed, but it will lack the elements of guilt, self-deception and role playing which contribute far more than genuine love to making bereavement destructive to the survivor.

In old age it is less these interpersonal forces than the collapse of mutual support and the disruption of a stable way of life, between people who didn't realize how much they supplemented each other, which are destructive, and resources are also less then to face such problems. Here help will be needed from family, friends and the senior community. If you can plan some structure of fallback for yourself, or for others who don't plan it for themselves, this is worthwhile and can bring some peace and comfort to a survivor that would otherwise be lacking. The kindest thing you can do for a bereaved person of any age is to be there, listen, support and show yourself open to his or her emotions. Do not hide because you don't know what to say. Saying should be avoided.

Blood Pressure. When I was a medical student, blood pressure was assumed to rise naturally with age. Modern medicine reckons that although it often does so, any such rise should be treated. It can be treated, and such treatment, even if it involves lifetime medication, is highly important, not only in protecting you against heart disease and stroke but because untreated rising blood pressure correlates with falling mental powers as time progresses.

Experimentation is afoot to lower blood pressure by using yoga-type relaxation and what is called biofeedback (self-training in controlling internal processes) instead of medication. Exercise also tends to lower blood pressure. But for the time being, the treatment is medication, which needs to be taken regularly and for an indefinite period. The time to start this is in early or middle life when the first rise is detected. Doctors have a battery of drugs, starting with simple diuretics, chiefly thiazides, which reduce the sodium load, through blocking agents, which also act as sedatives (propranolol), to stronger specifics used in more severe cases. Regular checking of blood pressure and the development of a strategy of treatment with your doctor is a highly sane preparation to avoid illness later in life. Low-sodium diets aren't usually necessary.

Some drugs which are used to treat high blood pressure have side effects. The common side effects, such as dizziness on standing up or getting out of bed, you are likely to report; the only one often not reported is interference with potency. This is not a usual effect, and is limited to some of the stronger drugs, but if you encounter it, talk to your doctor with a view to changing the type of medication you are taking.

It is obvious that you cannot lower blood pressure very much without interfering with its regulation, and most drug therapies carry a risk of dizziness on change of posture, especially when you begin them. You may, accordingly, have to learn to stand up, or get out of bed, slowly, and avoid stooping.

Treatment of slight and moderate high blood pressure is chiefly a preventive step, to be taken in early and middle life. At very high ages it may not need treatment, and the side effects of giving medication may outweigh the risk of leaving well enough alone.

High blood pressure starting in youth (and sometimes attributed to stress effects in the culture, although without much evidence) seems to be getting commoner, so most doctors check at all ages. It is particularly a threat to blacks in America, possibly because they are under even more stress than whites or possibly for other reasons as yet unknown.

❛The evening of life brings with it its lamp.❜

Joseph Joubert

Bertrand Russell, British philosopher and champion of individual liberty, was one of the most influential thinkers of the twentieth century. In 1960, when he was eighty-eight, he resigned from the Campaign for Nuclear Disarmament to form his own far more militant Committee of 100. At the age of ninety he intervened with heads of state during the Cuban crisis and with the United Nations during the Sino-Indian border conflict. In his autobiography, the last volume of which was published in 1969, the year before his death, he summarized his personal philosophy: "Three passions, simple but overwhelmingly strong, have governed my life: the longing for love, the search for knowledge and unbearable pity for the suffering of mankind."

Karen, Baroness Blixen, the
supremely gifted short-story
writer, was Danish, but wrote
most of her books in English
under the pseudonym Isak
Dinesen. Her first book, *Seven
Gothic Tales*, was published in
1934, when she was forty-nine.
Shadows in the Grass, her last,
appeared when she was
seventy-six, one year before
her death.

Bloody-mindedness is a British Army term without an exact American equivalent. It subsumes feistiness, cussedness and orneriness, with overtones of heroic obstinacy in not being put down, in defying popes, presidents, priests, professors, pundits and people generally when defending your own patch and your own right to be yourself. Bloody-mindedness is the chief adaptive character of man, the quality which made Britain, and probably also America, great, and it is the ultimate resource of the senior person. "Do not go gentle," said the Welsh poet Dylan Thomas, "into that good night." Still less should you go gentle into a bread-line, into a rip-off nursing home or into a state of fatuous senior Uncle Tomism.

The bloody-minded person kicks shins, telephones the media, writes letters and takes the door frame with him or her when assailed by the forces of faceless society. If his or her mind is bloody enough, he or she is invincible and dies in his or her boots.

We all know people like this and should emulate them —if we did, we would be treated if not with respect at least with fireproof gloves. It may not square with our ethic of good citizenship to be a kind of human poison oak, but the ethic has been largely devised to make us biddable, and we need have no qualms. Bloody-mindedness is an index of self-respect, and the most bloody-minded, in that they speak also on behalf of others who are more timid, are often the gentlest and most principled. Try forcing a Quaker to act against conscience and you will see what I mean.

Brain. The human brain does not shrink, wilt, perish or deteriorate with age. It normally continues to function well through as many as nine decades. If brain shrink-age or any of the other folkloristic changes were timed by the calendar, Artur Rubinstein at eighty-six would not have played better than he ever did, nor would Bertrand Russell at ninety have been conducting bitter public debates with President Lyndon Johnson.

There are two types of condition in which the brain does indeed deteriorate with time. One is interference with its blood supply. This may occur suddenly, as a "stroke" which, if it is not fatal, can be damaging. But such a sudden event doesn't as a rule impair intellect so much as function; it may upset speech, or cause paralysis. Since the side of the brain controlling speech is determined by handedness, ambidexterous people never lose their word sense as the result of stroke—they have, as it were, a "spare" speech area. The effects of strokes are quite often recoverable. Slow interference by hardening or closure of arteries, some outside the skull, causes most of the symptoms usually referred to as "senility" if these are physical in origin. It can be minimized by early prevention of high blood pressure, and can be quite strikingly halted by certain drugs, especially those which reduce clotting. If the oxygen-transport capacity of the blood could be boosted it might be recoverable, although the outcome of attempts to do this with high-pressure oxygen are controversial. If much of the problem arises from spasm (of the kind younger people get during the start of an attack of migraine, when they, too, can temporarily get interference with sight and speech), the dulling is intermittent and can be relieved by antispasmodic drugs, although not very reliably yet.

The other source of brain damage at late ages is a group of poorly understood diseases reflected in shrinkage and cell loss. Some of these appear in the fifties and are recognized as diseases. Those occurring later have been lumped together as senility, but are diseases nonetheless. Many were thought to be genetic and do indeed run in families, but at least one can be transmitted to chimpanzees by brain injection; the most recent guess is that they are viral. They may arise from very slow-acting viruses in the nerve cells, which, since they are not renewed, are vulnerable to such long-term processes, or by a more complex route; viruses we once met and beat, such as the measles virus, may be long gone, but might have left in nerve cells the chemical equivalent of a tape cassette carrying the instructions for making virus protein. If at some stage in cell life this tape were to be played, our immune system, programmed to attack measles, might jump on the cell and kill it in error. This is the equivalent of accidentally playing the Israeli National Anthem in the Kaaba at Mecca because your tape recorder got switched on.

Dementia in old age is neither general nor common, but because it piles up in hospitals it is visible and frightening. Actually it affects only a small proportion of the old. About 9.9 per thousand people over seventy need psychiatric hospitalization for all causes, compared to 33 per thousand in the next lower age group, and this

46

includes not only organic brain diseases but alcoholism, depression and ordinary insanity as well. On this reckoning less than 1 percent of older people can expect to be or to become demented. Old people go crazy for three reasons: because of illness, because they always were crazy or because we drive them crazy. In the first group we need to include not only the major diseases of the brain but also quite transient and curable complaints like the acute infections, because, while it lasts, any physiological upset more easily produces confusion of mind the older we get.

Other things can, of course, cause brain damage. Alcohol is one, although it is said that there are more old drunks than old doctors. Loss of brain cells, often put at some figure like one hundred thousand per day, probably reflects not age damage but some programmed clear-out process; the figure is trifling anyhow, and massive loss is always due to disease. Now that brain damage is no longer considered a right and proper part of aging, some of these diseases are being characterized, and may be preventable.

Aside from research studies, drugs, too, are under trial. These include antidepressants (see *Gerontology, KH3*), drugs such as meclofenoxate which remove pigment from nerve cells where it accumulates (whether it does harm there is anyone's guess at present), drugs which purport to boost cerebral performance (the most discussed lately, magnesium pemoline, seems to have been a lemon) and, more interesting, perhaps, some relatives of the hallucinogen LSD, which produce not a freak-out or any other dramatic change, but simply a brightening of the backdrop of consciousness—the difference between a dull, wet morning and a bright, sunny one. These may be a cop-out, but, so long as we make age miserable, it is a cop-out older people could use. Straightforward geriatric medicine cannot cure all cases of declining brain function, but it can help a great many dramatically with anticoagulants and other medication and should eventually be able to prevent a good many of them.

Going out of your head, losing your memory or becoming "senile" is statistically an unlikely misfortune. The word "senile" itself is less a diagnosis than a term of abuse—you're senile if you make waves. That indicates only that your brain is still functioning and they haven't washed it for you.

6It's a man's own fault, it is from want of use, if his mind grows torpid in old age.9

Samuel Johnson

47

John Wayne, the victor in a
thousand fictional fights, was
fifty-seven years old when, in
1964, he met and defeated the
darkest of adversaries, cancer.
Five years later he won an
Oscar for his starring role in
True Grit. His career as an
actor spans fifty years and
more than two hundred films,
seventeen of them among the
greatest money-earners in the
history of the cinema.

Cancer. About one-third of all people die of, or with, a malignancy—after all, you have to die of something. Cancer is treatable and in many cases curable; the reason it frightens us more than equally lethal conditions, like artery disease, is that once it is diagnosed and found inoperable it sets a time limit. Fatal illness is never jolly and can't be talked around, but a few facts are in order.

Cancer is not more painful or more harrowing by nature than other diseases. In old age its course is nearly always less acute than in middle life, and it may be discovered only at postmortem. Many cancers which are not radically curable can now be "slowed down" to give five or ten extra years—at seventy-five or eighty this isn't far off a practical cure. Cancer insurance policies are often small-print-based schemes exploiting your irrational feeling that insurance will actually prevent something, and cashing in on your fear of cancer; nobody ever offers stroke insurance, which would be far more to the point, since strokes can disable you for years.

You can virtually defy one common cancer by quitting cigarette smoking, and you can get a better chance at others by regular medical examination. The "signs" of cancer (which don't prove you have it, but call for investigation) are lumps which weren't there before in breasts or other places, any sore which doesn't heal, changes in bowels or waterworks and bleeding from any orifice. All these are more commonly benign, but check them out. *Check any sudden change*, and anything you don't like the look or feel of.

Centenarians. According to present figures, roughly one per thousand babies born in 1975 could be expected to reach the age of one hundred. (Present figures are, of course, cross-sectional mortalities which may not obtain in 2075.)

Centenarians are an interesting group to observe in order to further our understanding of "aging." As a group they seem to have outlived old age, because far fewer show the disease processes and chronic disabilities seen during the two preceding decades, most of which kill people before they reach the century mark. The steady climb in mortality, which actuaries usually assume to go on exponentially with time, flattens for this group. Obviously selection is winnowing them, but even so they are commonly pictures of what "aging" alone, without intercurrent age-dependent disease, would be like. Belle Boone Beard, a Georgia sociologist, wrote a book in 1967 about several hundred reputed American centenarians. Granted that blind, demented or sick people don't respond to inquiries, these people were a remarkable bunch. For a start, questioned as to their health, 17 percent said "excellent," 39 percent "good," 33 percent "fair," 6 percent "poor" and only 3 percent "very poor." These centenarians were fully engaged in life—driving, working where they were permitted to work and scoring higher than average on the "social space" they occupy. (One claimed to be Jesse James, and said that he escaped while another corpse was buried in his place, but let that pass. Humor was another centenarian characteristic.) Centenarianism may be genetic or due to luck—it cannot prove whether "social space" is preservative or whether to occupy it one has to escape growing disability. But most people who have worked with centenarians have the impression of a psychosomatic component—that these are people who aged without illness because they never let the bastards grind them down. This is possible. The alleged centenarians of Abkhasia in the Soviet Union would seem to fit into the same slot. If the theory is true, centenarians in urban, old-age-hating cultures may become extinct or the "social space" of the older citizens may return to normal and they will multiply.

Michel Eugène Chevreul's one hundredth birthday, in 1886, was the occasion of history's first photo-interview. The camera of Paul Nadar, the pioneer photographer, captured for posterity the wise, good-humored face of one of the nineteenth century's most distinguished men of science. An authority on dyes, he discovered the process of saponification, leading to the development of the soap and margarine industries, published works on the history of science when he was eighty and on theories of matter when he was ninety-two.

Melquiades Ortiz was actively farming his land in the Himbres Valley in southwest New Mexico when he was 104 years old. In 1964, when he was 101, Mr. Ortiz, a committed soil and water conservationist, became involved in an ambitious five-year group enterprise plan to completely rehabilitate the San Lorenzo Community Irrigation System. He later signed a cooperative agreement to carry out a soil and water conservation plan on his own farm, where he grew alfalfa, grain and apples with the help of his horse and a walking plow.

Checkups are valuable at all ages to pick up developing problems you didn't know you had. A checkup will detect incipient high blood pressure, and, of course, evident disease such as diabetes. Since medical problems get commoner as time goes on, checkups are needed in age as well as earlier.

The best kind of checkup is that given by a good family practitioner (even if he has fewer gadgets than a specialist) because, besides this kind of garage-type rundown leading to defensive action, it can be combined with a life-strategy discussion. This is what a doctor working with a patient, as opposed to a mere health technician, ideally gives. Obviously he gives it best if he and you know one another well, which was easier in a nineteenth-century village than it is in a city, and it takes a fair slice of his time.

Older people are usually well or obviously not well. Checking can't invariably result in curative medication, but it can warn of many specifics which could be ruinous if left alone, like rising pressure in the eyeball which can be treated, but will produce blindness if it isn't. Many later-occurring diseases, such as arthritis, can't be cured, but can be controlled and greatly palliated, and you will need referral to a good hospital. A doctor who knows you will spot, say, deafness before you do, and look into it. If disabilities do occur, strategy and a frank talk about the probable future course are highly important, because although we rightly and wisely assume we shall stay at least as fit as we are, some of us don't.

Once we are old having a doctor who will visit, and who knows how to treat old patients and how they differ from young patients, can make all the difference between continued activity and total disaster. Fly like the plague from the kind of veterinary technician who thinks anyone over seventy is likely (without further cause) suddenly to become senile or crazy, who tells you to "expect" illness, in terms of passive contemplation, as the normal state of older people, or who dislikes the old. If you were a dog he'd have you put down. This may be a counsel of unreal perfection today, but work for it.

Creativity is an attribute officially scheduled, if we may use the expression, to decline with age since the work of writers such as the psychologist H. C. Lehman. The true picture is best seen, not by quoting the continued creativity of Verdi, Michelangelo, Picasso and Rembrandt, who might be exceptional, but by looking at what actually happens in a specific field, such as science. Brilliantly original ideas rather naturally occur most readily early in life, because even brilliantly original people have, as a rule, only a limited supply of them, unless like Pasteur they are into many fields. These brilliant ideas arise most easily when the subject matter is fresh, and the individual tends afterward, like Einstein, to spend a lifetime in developing them.

If we look at all Nobel laureates, the average age of their first major paper was twenty-five, but all those past seventy continued to publish, as against three of a

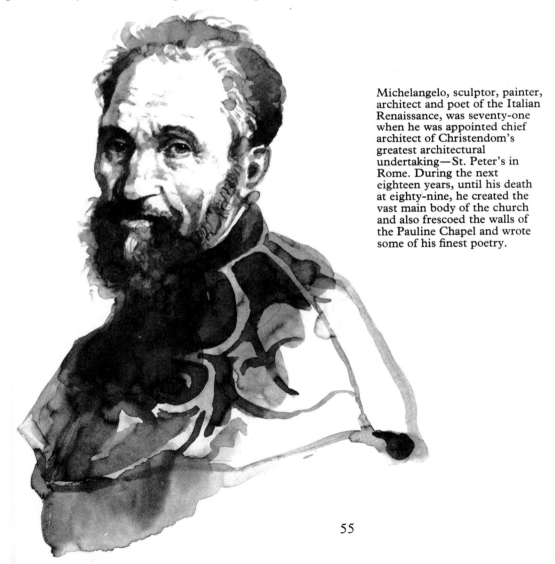

Michelangelo, sculptor, painter, architect and poet of the Italian Renaissance, was seventy-one when he was appointed chief architect of Christendom's greatest architectural undertaking—St. Peter's in Rome. During the next eighteen years, until his death at eighty-nine, he created the vast main body of the church and also frescoed the walls of the Pauline Chapel and wrote some of his finest poetry.

Pablo Picasso, one of the greatest and most influential artists of all time, remained to the end of his ninety-one years a man full of vigor and zest for life, working all day and often far into the night and exhausting younger companions with his unflagging energy and enthusiasm. His first exhibition, at sixteen, was followed by continuous and prodigious creativity which, in terms of sheer inventive inspiration, stylistic change, of volume and diversity of technique remained unparalleled. In seventy-five years he produced more than twenty thousand paintings, drawings, engravings, sculptures, constructions and ceramics.

matched group of nonlaureates. This could mean that papers by the eminent are never refused, but this does not appear to be the reason. The true reason is almost certainly that in science there is a self-fulfilling "career profile." A scientist moves out of research into administration, partly because unless researching is a consuming passion there may come a time when, as with football, he has played as much as he wants, and partly because, like Jefferson, scientists believe that

> *age is of course a fever chill*
> *that every physicist must fear:*
> *he's better dead than living still*
> *when once he's past his thirtieth year.*

Accordingly, they leave the field to "the young," who are supplied with a new crop of ideas, are, according to folklore, better at researching them and also, lacking status, are more ambitious; older men take the roles assigned them, of administrators, referees and gate-keepers.

This is perhaps no bad thing, for the reason that turn-over is, as Jefferson thought, good in itself, but the structure is imposed by causes other than some kind of built-in age deficit. Really good scientists work all their lives, and make one or more discoveries out of love of the game. The majority of scientists are journeymen; some have the originality to try a new tack in youth, because they and the subject matter are fresh. This is evidence not against later originality but in favor of second trajectories; if we cannot renew the man, we can renew the matter. Long-working artists know this; Renoir and Picasso were constantly changing their styles while a one-style painter like Chirico dried up early. Seniority in science tells against such continual updating—a physicist would usually rather switch to administering a physics program than to researching botany, but if he did turn to botany he would do so with interdisciplinary bases original in themselves. The picture we see in the organization of science illustrates well the unreal and the real in aging folklore, and the interplay of abilities with expectation, experience and life cycle. Change the expectation and the life cycle and you can expect an entirely different pattern of "originality"—which will not make unoriginal people creative, but could maintain the creativity of those who have the germs of originality within them.

Sonia Delaunay, the Russian-
born artist, always stood aside
in order to bring to the fore the
work of her husband, Robert,
who died in 1941. It was not
until 1953, when she was
sixty-five, that her exciting
work in many media began to
be exhibited internationally.
Her striking personal style
continued to evolve and she
kept extending her talents. In
her seventies and eighties,
as well as painting magnificent
abstract pictures she designed
tapestries, stained glass and
carpets.

Day Centers are a useful holding operation for the old, under present circumstances, and they offer the possibility of a far more useful and important operation than the original planners envisaged.

In the first instance, day centers were started by hospitals for sick old people, with the idea that they could attend them and get meals and treatment while able-bodied relatives were out at work, thus getting them out of the house and avoiding the need for a sitter. They proved immensely successful, and those which exist are a boon to people who would otherwise be stuck at home without company. The only problem with this arrangement, good as it is, is that elderly invalids have only the company of other elderly invalids. Therefore, many good hospitals started merging "old" day-attendance centers either with occupational therapy for patients of all ages or with a far more club-type operation which provided a clubhouse for ambulant and nonsick people, with meals at cost, and in cooperation with community volunteer operations, so as to mix the age groups.

When we can't immediately desegregate ages in this way, a senior club seems the next best thing or the first step, with the purely medical side as only one of its facilities. From this the club can branch out—often most easily to youth rather than to middle-age operations, for in our culture youth and age can very easily make common cause; they have problems in common against the rest of unconcerned society. One British day center and club enlisted Hell's Angels to run errands and drink coffee with the "old"—who, after they had been persuaded to open the door or to meet with "young hoodlums" in a club, ended by accepting some slow-speed rides on the boys' motorcycles, and letting them fix the roof or dig the yard, with social gain to both parties. Another good focus for a day center is a library and classes.

Death is the end of living, not the end of "old age," but obviously the longer we live the more realistically we are obliged to view it. It is something which, because it represents the end of experience, no normal person welcomes. Some cultures celebrate and in a sense "affirm" death, thus taking it into the sweep of experience. Our culture tends to deny or sentimentalize it, and push the deceased person out by the back door.

It is important to realize that only exceptionally is death itself painful, harrowing or tormenting to the dying person, nor is it the land-based equivalent of drowning. It is "that gentle thing which befell the maid-servant today and will befall the shepherd tomorrow." Not that that draws the teeth of dying. Our culture finds those diseases most intolerable which put us "under sentence of death" so that we know roughly when death will occur. Since these are commonly major diseases they are actually most frequent not in old age but in middle and late middle life.

Those who are in fact dying elect their own style of approaching the reality. Some prefer to ignore it and allow it to occur, on the basis that where death is, they are not, and where they are, death is not. More mature people welcome the opportunity to express to others their feelings, including resentment and anger, at human mortality. Nobody "needs to be told" that he or she is dying, but may be looking for an opportunity to tell you. This may be frustrated by your aversion or unwillingness to face such a situation yourself; this reaction is often the most trying thing a terminally ill person has to face.

Later life is not often preoccupied with death or dying (the late twenties are far more often so) nor need it be, beyond the scope of ordinary forethought and the protection of your relatives against speculative morticians. All that the "proximity of death" does to age is to add value to living, to reduce our tolerance of triviality and to increase our anger with those who, or those attitudes which, cause us to waste a store of time and experience that we cannot afford to dissipate or have destroyed.

> Old age hath yet his honour
> and his toil;
> Death closes all: but
> something ere the end,
> Some work of noble note,
> may yet be done,
> Not unbecoming men that
> strove with Gods.
> The lights begin to twinkle
> from the rocks:
> The long day wanes: the slow
> moon climbs: the deep
> Moans round with many
> voices.
> Come my friends,
> 'Tis not too late to seek a
> newer world.

Alfred, Lord Tennyson

Depression. In our culture old age can be an extremely depressing business, and depression in the underprivileged old is inherent in their situation. At the same time, depression is also an illness, accounting for much suffering at all ages. It is a particular hazard in later life because there is evidence that with the passage of time brain chemistry shifts in a direction which predisposes to mood changes, and because in mild forms depression may go unrecognized.

Acute depression may follow a reverse such as bereavement, when it appears as a deepening and an exaggeration of grief to the point at which it disables, or it may come on without warning, sometimes in recurring attacks which may alternate with excitement. Depression is the commonest cause of suicide at all ages, and may be aggravated by other sickness and social abuse in old age. While the acutely depressed person is seen to be ill and may recognize his or her state as illness, mild depressions, which are often long-lasting, may show no more than the loss of pleasure or reality in life, and may be interpreted by the sufferer as illness of a different kind. In old age, when life is often artificially unpleasant or unreal, and vague ill health may be attributed to "age," such mild depressions are generally missed altogether.

Pathological depression differs from grief in being— whatever set it off—a biochemical disorder affecting brain catecholamines. Most people suffering from acute depressions recover eventually by themselves if suicide is avoided. Minor or chronic depressions, however, can drag on for years, and in late life have an irrecoverable vicious-circle effect.

Medication can transform most depressions, and at earlier ages it is usually given. At later ages, and especially if it is assumed either by doctor or patient that old age should by nature be a miserable state, drugs may be withheld. Not a few geriatric depressions are themselves due to drugs (reserpine, methyldopa, digitalis, pro-cainamide, beta-blocking agents, barbiturates, alcohol or tranquilizers) to which late-life brain metabolism is, by young-adult standards, unusually susceptible. Tricyclic antidepressants are effective and safe, but, as with all drugs in later life, side effects are more idiosyncratic and commoner than at early ages, and require cautious dosage.

Loss of pleasure in life, of appetite, of libido, of sleep and of well-being are not features of aging. If you experience any of these without cause, you may require treatment for depression. The drill for the doctor is, naturally, to attack depressing features such as loneliness, bad housing and poverty in your environment to the best of his ability, but *also* to recognize that these, particularly loneliness, can in turn be effects as well as causes of depression. He will, accordingly, (1) inquire into, or reassess, all other medication which you are taking, (2) consider the use of antidepressants and (3) examine your general health—since after sixty-five factors like thyroid disease or vitamin deficiency sometimes trigger marked depression. Psychotherapy is usually only effective after these things have been taken care of, and, in the older person, centers on restoring some of the self-regard which society has destroyed.

Diabetes. This book is about age, not about specific diseases. On the other hand, diabetes gets commoner with age. So does "pseudodiabetes," a change in the rate of sugar removal from the blood which may be mistaken for the disease. This is an area where regular examinations pay, since even mild diabetes predisposes to cataract, gangrene, blood-vessel diseases and loss of potency. At high ages diabetes is often asymptomatic and is first detected when it causes one of these side effects. The best precaution is the regular checkup.

Dignity. Stand on this. (See *Pulling Rank*.) If other people don't recognize it, put them down—other older people depend upon the degree to which you ensure that anyone who thoughtlessly displays agism doesn't get away with it. React to people who talk slightingly about seniors ("old buffer," "old biddy," "dirty old man," "old lady in tennis shoes") in the way that black people have learned to react to people who talk slightingly about "niggers." Tell them you don't appreciate that sort of language. Your reaction will give them a salutary shock. Usually they mean no harm, but need their heads changed, to see older people as people, and only incidentally or secondarily as old. Don't put up with being addressed by nurses, aides and others as "Granny," "Pop" or the like. Point out acidly that you have a name and if they don't know it they can damn well ask, and that you were earning a living when they were still eating baby food.

Ordinarily thoughtless folk have learned not to parrot anti-Semitic, racist and otherwise socially poisonous phrases because both the persons they insulted, and decent citizens generally, rebuked them. It is high time to put agist remarks in the same "socially unacceptable" category. Never let "old" go past when it's used as a put-down. You could be good-natured and say that there's many a good tune played on an old fiddle, or that

❝Old age, especially an honored old age, has so great authority, that this is of more value than all the pleasures of youth.❞

Cicero

63

Mohandas Karamchand Gandhi,
India's great statesman
and spiritual leader, was sixty
years old in 1930 when he led a
two-hundred-mile march of
nonviolent disobedience against
the British Government's salt
tax. At seventy he undertook
a "fast unto death" and
compelled princely states to
grant democratic reforms. The
Mahatma was seventy-two
when he launched the Quit
India movement that led to his
country's independence in
1947, the year before his
assassination.

you're no older than they, you've only been around longer, but squelch the inclination. This is a part of the shaping of society—behavioral psychology teaches that if you alter people's verbal behaviors you alter them.

In entertainment, any time you see a senior depicted as a clown by virtue of age, pick up the phone. Even compliments can be left-handed. A feisty aunt of mine announced when she was eighty-five, "The next idiot who calls me a wonderful old lady, I shall clobber."

Age is venerable. It has earned esteem, however insignificant the aged person, by being around, by putting years into the work of society, by fathering or bearing the people who are doing the putting down. Words for "old" or "senior" gave us senator, elder, presbyter, guru and veteran. Don't you let anybody forget it; even if you don't have these titles, you belong to the club.

Disengagement is, in theory, the natural pulling up of tent pegs as we get older, and is a necessary consequence of decline. Long before Disneyland-sociology invented the word, it was expressed in 1561 with elegant melancholy by the Tudor translator, Sir John Hoby:

> *Therefore (me thinke) olde men be like unto them, that sayling out of an Haven, behould the ground with their eyes, and the vessell to their seeminge standeth styll and the Shore goeth: and yet it is cleane contrary—for the haven, and likewise the time & pleasures, contine still in their estate, and we with the vessell of mortalitye flying away, go one after another through the tempestuous Sea that swaloweth up and devoureth all Thinges; neither is it graunted us at any time to come on shore again, but alwaies beaten with contrary windes, at the end we break our vessell at some Rock.*

Disengagement in our culture is often, alas, sludge language for being ejected, excluded or demeaned, and liking it—an attribute wished on the newly created old to plaster our guilt and provide a piece of jargon to excuse our conduct. Age-proof people will have none of it.

If "disengagement" were real, it would have to be optional. In that case it would not be necessary to define it with a special name—at any age you can opt out of what you have been doing, often because it is seen to be not worthwhile.

Doctors. Age and death are two things with which many doctors have extreme difficulty in dealing. The reasons lie, probably, in the form of medical training which pitches the student into dealing with human suffering and decease without supplying much help in handling his feelings about them. After the initial shock, he finds that there are people he can help, and he develops an activist fantasy, of the St.-George-and-the-Dragon type, which serves as a shell. People who can't "get well" or who, by being old, exemplify a process which medicine cannot reach, are doubly castrating—by denying the fantasy and by reminding the doctor that he will get old and die, too. Some such process has to be invoked to explain the odd hostility of some medical people to the old. Another explanation is that geriatrics (being the study of old people who can't pay) has not been taught in American schools. Geriatrics is indeed as much a separate skill as pediatrics; older people react quite differently to drugs. They often get overmedicated out of their heads, and they have different symptoms. The pneumonia which in a baby will produce a fit, and in an adult an acute illness with fever and delirium, can appear in an old person with no symptoms, except confusion. If the doctor thinks that old people should expect to be confused, the patient may be put in a mental or chronic ward, when treating the pneumonia would clear the confusion in short order. There is today no more interesting branch of medicine than geriatrics. The intern who ignores an elderly patient with many symptoms as a "geriatric crumble" is abusing his vocation.

Such folk are rare; most doctors do an excellent job. From your point of view as a patient, the physician's attitude is the main thing to watch. Be suspicious if you are told that ill health is what you can expect at your age. Remember the man of 104 who, when he complained of a stiff knee, was told, "After all, you can't expect to be agile," and replied, "My left knee's 104, too, and that doesn't hurt." If you can find a physician who is actively into geriatrics, go to him or her. The only community with a really sound and ongoing attitude to geriatrics in America has been the Jewish community, which has some of the best geriatric hospitals. But as demand grows for active medicine in old age we can expect this attitude to spread.

Also, watch your own medication. Aging involves a multiplication in dysfunctions, minor and major, and this in turn involves an increase in the number of kinds of pill you may be given. You could find yourself with, for example, one pill for arthritic pains, a diuretic, a sleeping pill, some vitamins, one pill for heart rhythm and one pill for blood pressure. If it gets above four, check back with your doctor. Sometimes a busy prescriber is aghast to find a patient on ten or twenty pills, of which he has lost count.

Overmedication, especially with tranquilizers, is one of the commonest causes of blunting and confusion in older people. Of course, if you are going to second-guess the doctor all the time there is not much point in consulting him. On the other hand, this shouldn't be the relationship. If you have a really effective doctor, you will be able to discuss with him, get explanations and reassurance and jointly plan a strategy for tackling any of the inevitable problems of age. Ideally, you and he can do this looking at the future as well as at the present. If you are going to have problems seeing or getting around, it's as well to know in advance so that arrangements can be made, for example, to live where you can get to a store. And this sort of consultation is real medicine. In old age a good physician can be your most valuable ally.

If, on the other hand, you find someone who thinks that in the natural order you have to be infirm, crazy, impotent or the like, by virtue of chronological age, change doctors.

Since chronic sickness multiplies with age, old people are major—the major—consumers of health care; more than 70 percent of prescriptions are written for them. They need accessible medical centers, public transport which makes it possible to attend those centers, accessible walk-in clinics or mobile offices ("docmobiles") and doctors who make house calls. Of all citizens they most need a health service, preferably one based in community organization (the "healthy block") rather than in an elaborate centralized system which is governmental or insurance operated. The kernel of their management as patients and as people should be in-home care—whether by physicians or by physician assistants remains to be worked out. An old person is like an antique car—both require and repay careful maintenance. Such a service will be infinitely less costly than the alternative of waiting until disablement occurs and permanent, expensive and personally damaging institu-

6There is nothing more beautiful in this world than a healthy, wise old man.9

Lin Yutang

67

tionalization becomes unavoidable. On demographic grounds alone geriatrics is the growth stock of American medicine, and every old person should have access both to a primary-care physician, part of whose training has been in this specialty, and to a geriatric specialist for referral, backed by a geriatric assessment hospital of high standard. This will take time, and the return of the visiting family doctor is the first necessary step.

Drivers. Older, fit drivers are the least dangerous on the road. By seventy plus you have experience, and the accident-prone fraction of the population is dead or disqualified. There are only two real enemies of the older driver, aside from the conviction of some police and licensing authorities that he or she must be doddering; given a special test, most of us would do badly, knowing that our continued mobility was riding on it. Those real enemies are one which is obvious, bad sight, and one which is less obvious, acting out oldness.

A car is an extension of our body image. Older people often learn to walk deliberately, either through having painful joints and bad feet or through care to avoid falling or both. Once in a car these sensibly self-imposed limitations no longer apply, but an older person may then drive the vehicle "oldly" as if it was the body in question. Their driving becomes part of their usual non-verbal behavior, expressing lack of confidence in movement. But this is inappropriate and makes them drive too slowly in the middle of the road and position the car indecisively. If a following driver can spot from the nonverbal behavior of the car in front that the driver is old, as you could from his or her gait, then that older driver is already driving badly.

This aspect of driving is rarely stressed (it's assumed old folks drive indecisively *because* they are old). If you sense such behavior in yourself, take a few driving lessons to become aware that in the car you have a new, ageless body which you can handle with confidence and attack. You will vastly improve your driving by so doing.

It is possible that because of sight or for other reasons you will have to stop driving at some time. Reckon this one in your retirement strategy early. It's a knockout blow when it eventually happens if you don't have a backup way of living, especially in some areas where lack of transport makes car-less life virtually impossible.

6 Nothing is more dishonorable than an old man, heavy with years, who has no other evidence of his having lived long except his age. 9

Seneca

68

Aging does in fact slightly slow reactions. But in good older drivers this is fully compensated for by experience. There are men and women over eighty who still regularly fly private aircraft.

Drop Attacks affect a great many people of both sexes over the age of seventy-five. They are alarming and unpleasant, very frightening when they occur, but harmless provided you are not hurt in falling.

What happens is that while walking, sitting or standing, your legs give way and you fall. If you are walking or standing you may fall hard, and your main feeling on hitting the ground will be one of astonishment. Usually there is no "pass out" and clear memory persists of everything that happened. Strength returns to the legs almost at once. Apart from any injury, the main harm done is in sapping your confidence. These "bad turns" are usually not frequent, but they recur and produce a time-bomb effect.

Quite often, in typical drop attacks, the trigger is identifiable—for example, the quick turning of the head to an awkward angle or looking upward suddenly. If this is the case, the attacks can be cut down by avoiding the trigger movement or by wearing a neck support.

What seems to happen is that there is a momentary cutoff of blood to part of the brain, although why this doesn't produce ordinary fainting isn't clear. Probably the answer is that with age the large arteries in the neck become winding and are liable to kink, and a particular movement which kinks them, although it doesn't block the passage of blood, does upset the pressure sensor situated in the fork of the neck vessel, so it "turns off," as for an overload, and causes the blood pressure at the brain to fall.

If you get such an attack, check with your physician. Feeling faint after stooping isn't the same condition. Drop attacks are not strokes or fits and are, as we say, "benign." They don't herald serious illness. If you have many you will need a strategy to live with them, as epileptics live defensively in respect to things like open fireplaces and ladders. Constant worry about the next one can do more harm than the attacks. They are probably best defied.

Frank Lloyd Wright, America's
greatest architect, began his
most creative and prolific work
at the age of sixty-nine. It
ranged from the innovative
house, Falling Water, in Bear
Run, Pennsylvania, to New
York's circular Guggenheim
Museum, with its curving inner
ramp and tilting walls, which
was completed in 1959, the year
Wright died at the age of
ninety-one.

Albert Schweitzer, the great
humanitarian, was seventy
when, following the first atomic
explosion, he began working for
world peace. His appeals and
writings for this cause won him
the 1952 Nobel Peace Prize. Up
to the age of eighty-four he
visited Europe frequently and
lectured on the brotherhood of
man, and until his death at
ninety he actively cared for the
patients in his hospital at
Lambaréné, in Gabon. Doctor,
philosopher, theologian, writer
and musician, so sustained was
his capacity for all work that
at eighty-seven he helped build
half a mile of road near the
hospital, and then designed and
helped construct a stone bridge.

Education. The other face of agism is the concept of education which only "prepares young people for a career" and stops there. Education is lifelong.

Both the acquisition of new skills, including survival skills, and the lifetime experience of genuine education, are natural parts of the second trajectory of life. An ageless educational view of society will soon have the education industry rooting for it, since that industry is running out of children and of public credit at its performance in educating them.

Unemployed Welsh miners during the British depression of the twenties sometimes turned disaster into profit by using idleness to get educated. The unemployed American senior has better resources available than those miners had. Continuing or extramural courses, which cost money, admit seniors but are not yet comprehensively geared to the second-trajectory lifestyle; the media could help but are not used for this in America. At the same time, many schools and colleges have programs, not confined to yoga and macrame, in which you can enroll.

Education, along with defensive organization, should be a core component of any senior action center. One form, since nearly all unemployed seniors have skills, is the swap meet, at which crafts and languages can be exchanged. The ex-carpenter wants to learn Hebrew and visit Israel, the ex-rabbi wants to learn about investment, the ex-bank official wants to repair his roof, and these form a triangle.

Colleges approached by senior groups will often provide services voluntarily, if only the use of premises; sometimes they will provide the instructors. Classes can also meet around senior rights and the local situation, and move out into the creation of lobbying or registration groups. Whether you regard learning trigonometry or studying the stock market as your form of "education," some activity of this kind is inherent in the wish to stay alive and in the race, despite society.

Contrary to folklore, there is no change in the ability of healthy people to learn up to and beyond the ninth decade of life. Even languages are acquired as fast by healthy seventy-five- to eighty-five-year-olds as by high school students, although both acquire them more slowly than young children. There is strong evidence that, as with other capacities, using the mind preserves it.

> ❝It is always in season for old men to learn.❞
>
> **Aeschylus**

73

Anna Mary Moses, better known
as Grandma Moses, the
primitive painter, farmed in the
Shenandoah Valley and New
York State until her late
seventies. For many years she
had embroidered on canvas, but
when she was seventy-eight,
and her fingers became too stiff
to manipulate a needle, she
began to paint in oils. Her gaily
colored pictures of rural
America were soon being
exhibited internationally. In
1960, the year she was one
hundred, she illustrated an
edition of *'Twas the Night
Before Christmas*, which was
published in 1962, one year
after she died.

Erection is a major unnecessary worry (see *Sex*). The capacity for erection is never lost through age. It can become impaired by performance anxiety, medication, alcohol, obesity, diabetes and by thinking that it should become impaired. The only age changes are in the angle of the erect penis, which points down while in muscular youth it pointed up, and in the amount and character of the stimulation needed to produce it. In early life you often get "psychic" erections (from thinking about sex or from seeing a sexual object) whereas after about fifty this gets rarer (except in sleep) and erection may require two or three minutes of direct stimulation, by rubbing or otherwise, to bring it about. Both men and women need to know this.

The rules are: don't worry, don't hurry (in fact, continue the preliminary stimulation until the gear, like a nosewheel, locks in the down position—not "holding" erection is due to starting intercourse too soon) and check sudden changes in function to exclude the causes given above. If you ever get an erection (on waking, in sleep, at masturbation) there is obviously nothing wrong with the hydraulics. The commonest cause of sexual nonfunction at all ages is performance anxiety. You risk this if you treat sex as "performance." You can accelerate firm erection by finger pressure just behind the scrotum, by crossing the legs with pressure or by a tightish band around the base of both penis and scrotum. But these methods are for people in a hurry—adequate preliminary handwork, without hurry, is better for both partners.

Most, although not all, males of any age experience *some* unexplained periods of "running out of steam," lasting, if one dosen't get excited about them, at most four or five days. Even if this has happened before and they know through experience that it is temporary, people who are performance-obsessed often greet such a spell in later life as "the beginning of the end." More experienced lovers simply switch techniques and enjoy the variety, rather as many women do when they're having a period, using it to experiment with other forms of sex play. This may sound obvious, but half the males who have "given up sex because too old" aren't impotent at all, and 90 percent of the other half, who are "impotent," have absolutely nothing wrong with their hydraulics. You may opt out of sexuality because you wish to, or because you personally don't set much store

So, lively brisk old fellow,
Don't let age get you down.
White hairs or not
You can still be a lover.

Goethe

76

by it or are sick, but it's a pity to be psyched out of something you value by anxiety and wrong information.

If you need your confidence restored, mesterolone ("Proviron") may lower the stimulation threshold for erection. Few men with erectile difficulties are actually deficient in testosterone. Mesterolone can be useful in getting you functioning again, but it is experimental and needs medical prescription. Its advantage over male hormone is that it does not cause the central control mechanism to turn off your own, internal hormone production, as testosterone does.

Euthanasia. This is probably the most trumpeted non-issue of our time—so that by now many older people are scared out of their wits by the totally unreal prospect of being medically "buried alive"—kept alive, that is, in a vegetable condition by extraordinary medical means.

For a start, if they were in a vegetable condition they wouldn't know it, painful and expensive as that might be for relatives. Second, every decent doctor has had it drummed into him at medical school that the quality of life matters—that while he should never fail to try any kind of treatment which might restore a livable life, he is practicing bad medicine if he makes the treatment more grievous than the disease or uses what the Pope calls "extraordinary means" to revive someone only to suffer.

If we leave aside the pathologically depressed and those whom society has reduced to despair, few people of any age wish their end hastened, even if to us their circumstances look bleak or painful. There are exceptions, but as a rule *euthanasia is what the relatives clamor for*, not the patient. In fact, in the absence of proper geriatric teaching, far too many old people still get unwarranted euthanasia from doctors who reckon nobody over seventy is worth treating or that it's no use treating them. Quite a few of these not-worth-treating cases can take up their beds and walk, if anyone bothers to realize they are people and treats them accordingly.

In the present climate any further support for euthanasia would provide the super cop-out to express society's hostility against the expendable, not any act of mercy. As an administrative way of saving money, of not cleaning up the nursing-home racket, and of getting unwanted people to go away, euthanasia is a tailor-made solution. Older people who support euthanasia because of scare tactics are going along with this super cop-out.

Relatives who see "extraordinary measures" used beyond reason to keep a decerebrate person alive have a simple remedy—they can shut their checkbooks. The motives of such demeaning exercises are financial, not moral.

Exercise. The best sort of exercise in terms of retaining one's powers is the kind you don't call "exercise" or pay someone to arrange for you. The best exercise is work. Old-time pioneers or peasants don't "exercise." An old Swiss farmer doesn't exercise, he only walks four miles each way up and down a mountain to get to the store or to bring in his cattle. There's something a little off about fat, idle people riding stationary bicycles to lose the flab they got through overeating and overdrinking.

However, since we aren't all peasants, exercise is important. The problem is that it really needs to be lifelong, and that people of some body builds find it more enjoyable than others; for some people exercise is a real bore and doesn't produce a sense of well-being.

Starting violent unaccustomed exertion the day you retire is a good way of doing yourself an injury. If you've gotten that far without exercising and after being car-borne and desk-bound, a good gymnasium can indeed help—in which case start by trying the Y. Get a medical clearance first. Exercises to restore fitness, such as situps and other floor exercises, will get you into better trim for your post-retirement trajectory. Women and some men may prefer dance to drill, and both may prefer yoga. (Make sure you have a sensible, trained instructor. Don't go to classes started by friends, at least not in the first place.) All these approaches restore physical activity and decrease your heart rate and blood pressure. If you use yoga meditation for this, take some gym as well to improve your mobility.

Once fit, the best way to stay fit is to integrate exercise in your life-style by doing a job which includes it. If you can't arrange this, the best cheap exercise is walking, if you live where you *can* walk.

Nonexercise probably accounts for a great many age changes. In a study done for the Administration on Aging in 1968 by Dr. H. A. De Vries, a class of seventy-year-old men joined a one-year exercise program. They ended with the bodily reactions of men thirty years younger.

Duncan MacLean won a silver medal at the 1975 World Veterans' Olympics, in Canada, when he ran two hundred meters in forty-four seconds. He was then ninety years old. Scottish-born, Mr. MacLean was sprinting champion of South Africa from 1905 to 1907. He toured the world with a comedy song-and-dance act until the late 1940s. Then, in his sixties, he became a house painter. He retired when he was eighty, but continued sprinting, practicing daily at a training center near his London home and taking part in international athletic events. His ambition: "To run a hundred meters on my hundredth birthday."

Falls are the chief late-life accident menace. Because of increasing bone brittleness, a fall can easily lead to a fractured hip. Although this is mendable, any confinement to bed is harmful to a person over seventy, and the whole episode, especially if it leads to reduced mobility later, can trigger off a loss of pleasure-in-life which ends in death. Therefore, don't fall. The strategies are to avoid risks, ranging from walking on icy streets to being too proud to carry a cane, to light dangerous corners (see *Lights*); and if you have to negotiate, for example, garden stairs, to put in a handrail. Bathtubs are another pitfall at all ages, but especially for seniors because of the fracture risk. Put in a handrail here and use a nonslip insert. Do these things *before* you reckon you need them. Check stair carpets and carpet edges; look out for stools and pets.

Tripping is the commonest cause of falls, and turning suddenly the second commonest. If you fell without a cause or through suddenly blacking out or going weak this was probably a drop attack (see *Drop Attacks*), but in any case check with your physician.

Falling down and getting badly hurt is a common (and justified) fear of older people who live alone. Have a backup strategy for this emergency—someone who calls, or whom you call, at a set hour, a neighbor who checks if you picked up the newspaper or, if you can afford it, a help alarm. Some of these call assistance if you don't reset them from time to time. One kind is reset every time you flush the toilet and rings if you don't do so in eight hours. This is at least a backup security in case you hurt yourself or meet with any other emergency.

Nearly all harmful falls occur in the home, and nearly all occur as the result of tripping during normal activity, not while climbing ladders and the like. Don't of course live as if you're made of glass, but do check the security of what you stand on, take climbing slowly and move everything which you need often to shelves you can reach without climbing. It's an unfortunate feature of aging that what would have been painful in youth can be fatal in age.

Fear of the supposed necessary effects of aging is a major cause of "aging" as a social disability. At the same time, there are things of which it is prudent to be afraid.

The chief *reasonable* fears are of ill health, of poverty, of being the victim of attack or robbery, of falling and of becoming ill while alone. Unreasonable fears (fears, that is, laid on us by old-age role prescription) include fear of losing grip or memory, of being a burden, of making demands and of "losing our dignity" by insisting on public entitlements for which we have paid. It would be a charitable view that these fears have grown up, like Topsy, rather than been deliberately fostered to manipulate older citizens into a cheap, quiet and invisible existence.

Poverty is a real worry (see *Poverty*), so is falling into the hands of a "nursing home"; you could profitably, if you are not poor, disinherit your heirs if they permit you to be placed in one. Fear of emergencies when alone can best be met by having an alarm or checkout system in operation (see *Falls*) plus "delethalization" of your house—which means, in decent English, doing away with hazards—and reasonable, though not terrified, care in movement.

Crime against the old can't be met except by locks and suspicion, unless older persons become a lobby strong enough to harass public authorities for action, better street lighting and protection. Guns are a bad idea unless you have the skill and determination to use them, and they cause more tragedies than they prevent.

All fears can be lessened by sensible action if that action is taken by seniors collectively. The biggest fear is of being on one's own, without resource. But 22 percent of the electorate need only be without resource so long as they fail to come together.

Feet. With the coming of age, you get to appreciate your feet—just about the time when years of injudicious footwear and weakening ligaments catch up with you.

Chiropodists and doctors rightly advise people to double-check and care for their feet in later life (especially if they have diabetes or bad circulation), ignoring the fact that this is just the time of life when it gets harder to get at them—either because of stiffness or because stooping, to cut nails, for example, makes you dizzy. Also good shoes cost money, and many hard-up oldsters "make do" to their hurt.

One valuable feature of any senior club or day-attendance center can be a podiatry parlor. Some people I have seen grew long toenails like unshod donkeys because they couldn't reach to cut them and were embarrassed to ask friends for help. Any two people can clip

❝We do not count a man's years, until he has nothing else to count.❞

Ralph Waldo Emerson

81

one another's nails, but it should be done in a good light, so as not to produce overcuts which may become septic and start trouble.

As with everything else, the time to take care of feet is early in life, by avoiding freak shoes and by exercising. If you have painful feet, consult a physician. "Good feet and a good bowel" are part of the equipment for senior vigor, and neither fashion nor pavements nor standing do anything to produce feet which will last.

Fertility. Female fertility ends at the menopause. The only practical problem here is that if you are on the Pill, or on some other hormone regime, and aren't sure if you have stopped ovulating, you can, on stopping the Pill, get surprisingly pregnant if your guess was wrong, a bad thing to happen because you don't need a baby in middle life and because at about the premenopausal age the risk of mongolism in the fetus increases.

Fertility is lifelong in many men, lasting into the nineties. Men who become spontaneously infertile usually do so much earlier in life. A sperm examination can settle this. Unlike motherhood, age doesn't bar fatherhood, since there is no evidence that the progeny of old fathers runs any health risk. After all, sperm are short-lived and newly made, whereas all the ova a woman will ever have are present when she is born. If you are very old you should, however, consider that in the course of nature you may not be around for the whole period of fathering, which includes adolescence. You need a probable run of sixteen years to see the job through, which rules out responsible procreation after about seventy if this argument governs you. Assuming it does, and you have a fertile partner, you won't let age make you sloppy about contraception. Vasectomy is perfectly in order for older males with live sperm at test. It does not affect potency, and was formerly done, under the name of Steinach's operation, as a rejuvenatory procedure; there is not much evidence that it rejuvenates, but it certainly does no harm.

Men have fathered children at least into their nineties and possibly older. Fertility in women is theoretically possible so long as menstruation continues, but births at ages over fifty are rare. The oldest mother credibly recorded was a Mrs. Ruth Kistler of Los Angeles, who reputedly had a daughter at the age of 57 years and 129 days.

82

Fires are a significant hazard to older people because they lack agility, and because in later life people are easily rendered unconscious by smoke. Fires are obviously particularly dangerous to the sick old in institutions (a good many of which make profits at the expense of fire-department regulations) or in poor housing—run-down hotels or small rooms with ancient wiring. Fires may start because older people feel the cold and leave antique heating appliances on, but one of the commonest causes is still smoking in bed and falling asleep. This risk has been increased by polyurethane cushions and mattress pads, which rapidly generate large amounts of toxic fumes when lit. Fumes and smoke, not fire, kill most fire victims.

Tighten up your fire precautions in later life. If you have relatives in "nursing homes" and care about their survival, persistently harass both the proprietors and the fire department about fire precautions. In your own home the major traps are flammable furnishings, plastic ceiling tiles and heaters at or near floor level, which are capable of igniting clothing. Overloaded electric outlets and kerosine heaters are others. Check your escape routes and make sure you can negotiate them. This applies at any age, but fires kill more older people and more young children than any other groups.

Flying. There is absolutely no reason, if you have the money, why you shouldn't fly as a passenger at any age. It's a lot less wearing than the bus, and the airline will usually look after you.

Unless you are very active, swallow your diffidence and pull rank to make sure there is a cart to convey you to the plane from the checkout counter (it can be as much as a mile). If in doubt tell them you are an invalid, which they'll at least understand. The main snag if you tire easily is the possibility of a long cancellation delay or a midflight turnback on a long journey. If you've shaped the airline properly by phone before leaving home, however, you still may have a whale of a time regardless. If you don't get the treatment your seniority demands, thump on some desks or appeal for sympathy, depending upon how assertive you are, and if that fails, faint. Usually this isn't necessary. Afterward a letter of appreciation to the airline can guarantee a repeat performance on the way home.

❛As a man advances in life he gets what is better than admiration —judgement to estimate things at their own value.❜

Samuel Johnson

83

Nadia Boulanger, born in Paris
in 1887, for more than fifty
years taught musical
composition. Her students
included many of the twentieth
century's leading composers.
When she was fifty-one years
old she appeared as the first
woman conductor of the Boston,
New York Philharmonic and
Philadelphia orchestras. When
she was sixty-three she became
director of the American
Conservatory in Fontainebleau.
In 1975, at the age of eighty-
eight, still teaching and
frequently traveling abroad to
judge international music
competitions, she appeared in a
television program celebrating
the seventy-fifth birthday of
Aaron Copland, one of her
distinguished students.

84

Folklore and Nonsense. Probably the best remedy for these is cold fact. Here are a few of the leading examples concerning age. A surprising number of people, including administrators, believe them. Test yourself. True/false.

Most old people live in institutions—hospitals, homes, etc.
The actual figure is just under 4 percent for all persons over sixty-five.

Most old people are constantly in bed because of illness.
They get fewer acute illnesses than younger people: 1·3 illnesses per person per year as against 2·1 for all ages. True, 81 percent of people over sixty-five have some chronic problem, as against 54 percent of all people below that age, but this need be nothing worse than short sight or hay fever.

After sixty-five everyone goes steadily downhill.
In the Duke University longitudinal study, 44 to 58 percent of survivors over sixty-five who returned for checkups had *no* detectable deterioration in physical condition, and some had improved, over periods from three to thirteen years. True, some people do suddenly get sick and decline, but this can happen in earlier life and is called illness, not aging. For all people over sixty-five, 51 percent rate their health as good, 33 percent as fair and 16 percent as "poor." About half, or possibly more than that, of any decline that is observed, is due to boredom, inactivity and the awareness that infirmity is expected.

Old people are typically alone, abandoned by family and lonely.
In the United States 80 percent of people over sixty-five live with someone else; 75 percent say that they are "not often alone" and 86 percent saw one or more relatives during the previous week, according to a typical study done by Dr. Ethel Shanas. She also charted proximity of nearest child to oldsters who had one; for 2,012 people over sixty-five it ran: 28 percent live in the same house, 33 percent live ten minutes away or less, and another 23 percent live within an hour's travel away. It doesn't of course follow that none of these people is lonely or neglected, but the stereotype is clearly way off. (See *Loneliness*.)

6If I did not keep telling myself my age over and over again, I am sure I should scarcely be aware of it. Although every hour of the day I tell myself "My poor old fellow, you are seventy-three and more," I cannot really persuade myself of it.9

André Gide

86

Dr. Malley Kachel of Munich never considered retiring or even taking life easy. At the age of ninety-four, the oldest still-practicing woman doctor in Germany, she continued to look after her devoted patients.

People should retire; older people can't do a decent job.
Quite apart from knocking this statement down with serried ranks of artists, musicians, writers and other brands of intellectual who have done good work until they dropped, it's more to the point to stress that such persisting usefulness is *the rule*, not a privilege of genius. There is a slight *positive* relation between industrial productivity and worker age, and older workers have a 20 percent better absenteeism record than younger workers. They also have fewer disabling and non-disabling injuries, and the frequency of accidents decreases with age. At this point convention decrees that we stop employing them.

Everyone knows old folks are past having sex.
Every study shows that a high proportion of old folks

are either still having it or would welcome an opportunity to have it because they are fully able to enjoy it. (See *Sex*.)

After sixty-five your mind deteriorates and you can expect to get senile.
In fact the only thing that declines a little is speed of response; there is no change, normally, in intelligence and little in memory. Any blunting we do see in the absence of actual disease commonly results not from age but from put-downs, boredom and exasperation. About 1 percent of all people become "demented" or "senile" —less than the percentage who go insane at earlier ages. (See *Intelligence*.)

Old folks spend all their time sitting around watching television.
So would you, if you were put out of work and prevented from getting any; however, people over sixty actually spend less time watching and listening to the media than people in their twenties. The Duke study found no significant fall in people's activities at ages from sixty to ninety over a ten-year period—those who had them kept them.

Louie Dingwall, a grandmother and the trainer of many winning racehorses, was seventy-nine years old when she announced her intention of applying for a license to ride in women's races. When she was eighty-two, on the first day of the 1975–6 English National Hunt season, two of her horses won the first and second races and another was runner-up in the third.

Disengagement is a natural acceptance of old-age limitations—older people really welcome it.
Sometimes. More often it's a sugarcoated way of covering up for our guilt at easing out the people we want for other reasons to treat as disposable, and belongs to the sludge language of commercial sociologists. In plain terms it means "people really like being kicked out of the living community, put to grass or treated like lepers—because if they made waves about it, that would be inconvenient for our planning." Like plantation slaves enjoyed being slaves, remember? After all, it was for their own good.

Since physical aging is a natural process, it can't be altered.
In animals the rate can be halved. Whether anything similar is possible in man is being studied. (See *Gerontology*.)

Most of the handicaps of older people are physical; after all, they are old.
Most of the handicaps of oldness in our society are social, conventional and imaginary. The physical changes are trifling by comparison. Old age as we see it exists only in societies which create it by the way they classify people, and it could be abolished tomorrow by declassifying them (leaving some time to debrainwash everyone after that).

Who believes this nonsense anyway?
Unfortunately, quite a lot of younger people, and some older ones for whom it's a big source of anxiety, because they expect to suffer the various changes it conjures up for them. When they reach age and find they don't they're agreeably surprised and think themselves exceptionally lucky. It's interesting to notice that people who, as it were, militantly believe that the old are subhuman, rather than having picked up the idea as a background radiation in the culture, are the people who also think badly of invalids, foreigners, Jews, Negroes, Italians, workers, the unemployed and hot-dog-stand proprietors—in other words they are prejudiced against every group of people they can identify and some they wouldn't know if they saw them. It's not this sort of redneck bigotry which hurts the old, however. It's the steady drip of precisely the misinformation we've been describing that prepares people to be victimized at sixty-five and

6 Intelligence, and reflection, and judgement, reside in old men, and if there had been none of them, no states could exist at all.9

Cicero

the rest of us to help victimize them until we get there ourselves. It's a nice point in the conspiratorial theory of history how far the spreading of such erroneous ideas is due to sheer accident and misunderstanding, and how far people foster them out of self-interest; probably here it's the first—wasting 20 percent of the population doesn't seem to be in anyone's interest, especially since everyone eventually joins that 20 percent.

Food, like sex, is one of the pleasures that stays with us all through our lives. The idea that old people live on pet food and dry bread has little to support it statistically—those who do are the depressed, the anemic, the impoverished and the sick. In Britain at least, and probably in America, evidence suggests that sickness more often produces malnutrition (through loss of appetite and not caring) than malnutrition produces sickness. Only 3.2 percent of people over sixty-five were clinically malnourished according to British studies, and figures for America are apparently similar.

In later life, most people have fewer teeth and less saliva than formerly, but even the old who dislike or do not get dentures remain remarkably well able to chew, and disdain pap of all kinds. Proper dentures are, however, an asset, and it is worth persisting until they fit. This may mean fairly frequent revision, as the mouth may change rapidly in later life. Not having good dentures also makes you look senile, by producing "nutcracker" features.

Most of the damage done to health by diet has been done before we reach seniority. In fact, the foundations of obesity probably get laid in babyhood, and those of artery disease not much later. Calorie restriction prolongs life in almost all animals (see *Gerontology*) and might do so in man, but a suitable human diet has not yet been tested. The guidelines at the moment are to avoid weight gain while taking an adequate calorie and protein intake (around 2,300 Calories a day for a man and 2,000 for a woman at age seventy to seventy-five) and avoiding excessive animal fats and cholesterol. This last means adhering to the American Heart Association's prudent diet (see page 215), which substitutes vegetable margarine for butter (note the list of ingredients on the package: "liquid corn oil" or "liquid safflower oil" should be the first listed—otherwise you might as well eat butter). The diet also bans cream, fat bacon and fat

❛Youth ended, I shall try
My gain or loss thereby;
Be the fire ashes, what
    survives is gold:
And I shall weigh the same,
Give life its praise or blame;
Young, all lay in dispute; I
    shall know, being old.❜

Robert Browning

meat of all kinds, as well as lard, and limits eggs to two a week while going easy on liver and shellfish. It often pays to get a written diet, because this suggests dishes and lays out a program, but avoid all gimmicks. By the time you reach sixty-five your chief need is for a mixed but balanced diet.

In a country with abundant fresh vegetables you shouldn't need vitamin pills, which are an incredibly expensive way of getting things you can get from food. Vegetables also provide fiber, which is a cure and prevention for many late-life diseases of the gut and a preventive of constipation; fiber also appears to lower blood cholesterol. Constipation is an imaginary disease at most ages, with the emphasis on the con, but in old age the bowel may get sluggish if the diet lacks fiber for the muscles to work on. Bran, plain or processed, is an excellent source. Instant protein supplements are both expensive and bad for morale, because you get used to living on liquids and stop cooking. Keep them for emergencies.

The nutritional danger times in later life are the periods of depression, of sickness or of bereavement. Most people of all ages look forward to meals, although the alone and the lonely may stop bothering to prepare them as part of a general *accidie*. It takes willpower to eat properly at such times, but if you don't the process is circular and you lose ground, perhaps irrevocably.

Studies—unsurprisingly—indicate that old people who are not otherwise sick need exactly the same foods as other people, although in slightly less quantity if they are not strenuously active, and they have the same vitamin deficiencies as are seen in the global population. Food technology could help brighten Meals-on-Wheels for those who can't readily shop or cook, because it could produce quality frozen foods which need little preparation and are interesting enough to make eating an event.

You don't, therefore, need to change your diet as a result of the passage of years, unless it was a diet you should have changed anyway. The problems arise with poverty, illness, depression or practical difficulties in getting the ingredients for meals—steep stairs, for example, or a neighborhood where you dare not go out. None of these has simple answers, but at least you can recognize that a falloff in your enjoyment of food at any age is a bad sign, and indicates that the warning light for getting help is on.

George Bernard Shaw, who is considered the most important British dramatist since Congreve, wrote his first play when he was thirty-six years old. Art, music and drama critic, novelist, author of tracts and books on socialism, as well as playwright, Shaw's last produced play was written when he was in his late eighties. A vegetarian, he remained vigorously productive until his death at ninety-four.

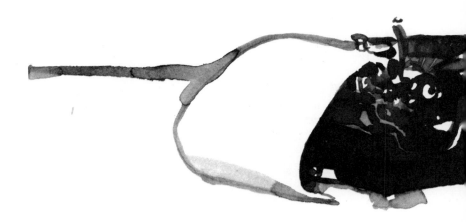

Very enlightening
really enjoyed reading
this book. Thank
you so much.

Dorothy Heft

Bentyl®
(dicyclomine hydrochloride USP)

Merrell

Fountain of Youth. A nice legend, best laid out by Rabelais. It is chiefly of interest to Americans because Ponce de León was looking for it when he came from Europe. What he found instead was the state of Florida. Probably the nearest approach to the fountain of youth is the jacuzzi, or the California hot tub. These small, sociable whirlpool baths don't "rejuvenate," but they are stunning icebreakers at any age. And they reveal the fact that many older people—since uncovered skin ages faster than covered skin—still have good bodies they needn't be afraid to show. Luckily even Mickey Mouse morals don't insist we wear clothes in our bath, and communal bathing is a minor bonding experience at all ages. To that extent it "rejuvenates." In Japan it is a general recreation.

Genetics. Long, healthy life does indeed run in families. Raymond Pearl, the founder of American actuarial statistics, long since showed that one of the best preparations to live in health to a high age is having four long-lived grandparents. The workings of longevity genetics are interesting. One big component is not what you inherit, but what you don't—the absence of genetic traits tending to "shortevity"; there are, for example, families in which early heart attacks are common. Another component is something called overdominance, or hybrid vigor—the second name comes from farming and from laboratory mouse breeding. Here, if two pure, unlike strains are crossed, the first generation offspring are not only larger, fitter and faster growing than the parents but are also longer lived. In both man and horses, there is a correlation between the longevity of parents and children, but it is only one-eighth the correlation for stature; it is much smaller than the correlation between siblings, which suggests that overdominance operates.

It's sometimes asked, purely as an exercise, if we could breed long-lived people. The answer, based on work with animals (which is incredibly tedious, even with fruit flies, since you have to wait out their life span, keeping all the offspring), is that selection boosts longevity initially by removing shortevity traits, but after this the life span plateaus and then falls off through inbreeding. The best bet to "breed" a long-lived human

6 There was Pantagruel told by the keeper of the fountain that it was his wont to recast old women, so making them again young, and by his art to become like to the young wenches there present whom he had that very day recast— and altogether restored to that same beauty, form, size, elegance and disposition of limbs, as they had displayed at the age of fifteen or sixteen years, save only in regard to their heels, which were somewhat rounder than in their true youth. For this reason from thenceforth upon meeting a man, they were apter to fall on their backs. The band of old women attended upon the next round of recasting in great devotion and zeal, and importuned him on every hand, saying that it was a thing in nature intolerable if a willing piece of tail lacked the looks to match. Pantagruel asking him by remelting and recasting old men might likewise be remade, he answered that they could not, but that for them the manner of rejuvenation was by commerce with a woman renewed. 9

Rabelais

94

would be to persuade an Eskimo to marry an Australian aborigine, in the hope that their gene pools would be widely different and would give the children an unusually good hand of cards. Inbreeding steadily lowers vigor by all indices, while miscegenation improves it, often strikingly.

The usual assumption is that longevity depends at this level upon a good and varied hand of cards with no bad-luck cards included. It is also just possible that there are some specific genes for unusually long life, which affect such things as rate and behavior of brain clocks. There is absolutely no evidence yet, but it has been suggested as one explanation of pockets of purported supercentenarians in places like Vilcabamba in Ecuador, or Abkhasia in the Soviet Union. Aside from the fact that the real ages of these people are in dispute, diet, exercise, continued activity and isolation from viruses are equally possible; they all live in remote mountain valleys where there are no towns, few tourists and often no birth certificates. A longevity gene group which enabled one to reach the age of 120 would be a little like the gene group which makes nearly all the African Wa-tutsi seven feet tall, and gives us a lot of tall basketball players who had Wa-tutsi ancestors. If such a group affecting longevity did exist, we don't know if it would be an all-or-none effect, or, like most stature genes, a continuous variable.

Nobody is about to "breed" long-lived, or any other, people, and we ourselves have been bred already and must make do with the genes we have. Even given a downer like a known family predisposition to heart attacks, at least you have a warning—and can take check-up precautions with a better chance of success than a person who has no reason to expect trouble, and who neglects such things as sane diet. Dementia in old age was formerly considered "genetic." Quite possibly it is viral and resembles the virus disease scrapie in sheep, which only attacks sheep of certain kinds. Genetics doesn't mean, then, that we have to take what comes to us—it can actually brief us on possible preventables.

❝When I was young I was amazed at Plutarch's statement that the elder Cato began at the age of eighty to learn Greek. I am amazed no longer. Old age is ready to undertake tasks that youth shirked because they would take too long.❞

W. Somerset Maugham

Age only matters when one is aging. Now that I have arrived at a great age, I might just as well be twenty.

Pablo Picasso

Gerontology. If you live in an economically privileged country, you have a good chance of living to become "old" and of dying at an age between seventy and ninety, or higher. In fact, apart from war, accident, pollution and bad repercussions from food and smoking, most people now die of "old age." This really means that they die of age-dependent diseases—those which become commoner in later life—plus the general decline with time in the body's capacities for self-maintenance and quality control. It is this decline which, for the biologist, constitutes aging. In all organisms which age, aging expresses itself as an increased liability to die with the passage of time.

The rate at which this kind of aging occurs is set for each individual species, and gives each species its characteristic life span. Man is probably the longest-lived mammal. His rate of aging is such that "old age," characterized by gray hair, skeleton and muscle changes and increased susceptibility to illness, is evident around age seventy-five in most people, giving us a life span, or commonest age of dying from natural causes, of between seventy-five and eighty years. The curve has a "tail" extending to the maximum recorded human life span, which cannot be given with certainty but is probably short of 120 years, 111 to 112 years being well established by birth certificate. These are ages which represent a signal combination of good luck and good genes.

People now live longer than they did a few years ago. This is wholly due to the suppression, by medicine and prosperity, of deaths occurring early in life. The mean length of life (arrived at by adding up all the lives and dividing by the number of people) in 1760 in Germany was 34·5 years. In 1830 in Sweden it was 41·5 years, and by the turn of the century it reached 57 years. According to 1972 figures, in the United States it was 68·3 for white males, 76 for white females, 61·3 for black males and 69·9 for black females.

These figures have absolutely nothing to do with the control of aging. "The years of Man are threescore and ten, or by reason of strength fourscore years," wrote the biblical author. They still are, only more of us reach them. Those who do so "get old" at exactly the age that Moses and Pharaoh "got old." Medicine has done nothing whatever to alter the human life span, but it has been strikingly successful in making us live to the end of it. Between 1900 and 1948 the expectation of life of

American males at birth went up from forty-eight to sixty-five years. The expectation of life at sixty went up by one year. It has gone up about another year since then, and these increments are entirely due to some non-deaths attributable to such advances as antibiotics and better surgery.

The truth is that by getting most of us through to seventy, medicine has just about shot its bolt, and there is little chance that the cure of further diseases on a one-off basis will greatly extend our lives. The reason for this is that the vigor loss in age is general, and is expressed as a multiplication of causes of death. It has been calculated that the radical removal of our three leading causes of death—heart and blood-vessel disease, brain-vessel disease and cancers—would put about seven years on the overall expectation of life by preventing early deaths, but perhaps not more than two and a half years

Margaret Mead, doyenne of social anthropology and one of the founders of psychological anthropology, made a field trip in 1973, at the age of seventy-two, to restudy the Arapesh people of New Guinea—some forty-eight years after her very first expedition. In 1975 a television film traced a typical week in her life, including a two-seater flight to a Navajo Indian reservation. It was a week so packed with work that it would have exhausted anybody half her age.

on the expectation at age sixty-five. If doctors examine the body of a person who dies of illness at forty they normally find one cause of death; in a person dying at ninety there are likely to be twelve or thirteen causes, any one of which would eventually have been fatal.

An "ideal" survival curve can in fact be drawn in which nobody dies, except by accident, before age sixty-five, and everyone is nevertheless dead by age 110, with deaths occurring most commonly around eighty. The pattern in privileged countries is already pushing this limit. Once reached, we are up against a natural "brick wall," so far as curative medicine directed at single

Leo Tolstoi, the great Russian writer, experienced a spiritual conversion at the age of fifty-one. Thereafter, moral, social and anarchistic themes pervaded such works as *The Death of Ivan Iliych*, completed at fifty-six, and, at seventy-two, *The Resurrection*, the income from which he gave to a pacifist sect persecuted by the government. Among some of the most poignant of his works were those written during the few years before his death, at the age of eighty-two, including the posthumously published *I Cannot Be Silent*, which attacked the government for executing revolutionaries.

diseases is concerned. We would simply die soon after of something else (rather as when, in an old radio, you replace a component which has burned out, you restore the voltages to what they were when the set was new and something else blows). Aging is the process which affected the Wonderful One Hoss Shay.

There are diseases of age which can be palliated, both by skilled medical treatment and by such less popular maneuvers as treating older folks decently and giving them enough money to live on. It could also be that a radical prevention of, say, blood-vessel disease, might have a greater effect on health than has been computed. The improbably old peasants in various areas who claim to be 140 or 150 and are probably a vigorous 100, give or take a few years, seem to owe much of this vigor to being free of arteriosclerosis. But if we want to *alter* the human life span, not just reach it, no antibiotics, artificial hearts or other kinds of high-investment technology can do more than produce a law of diminishing returns.

If aging were an invariant laid down in the nature of things, like the velocity of light, we would probably better accept it with dignity and spend our energies on improving the quality of the eighty-year span which we have got. In point of fact aging is not an invariant. "Aging" is a biological process involving a rate or rates, and where there is a rate it can generally be altered. This is now the assignment of experimental biology. In fact, the rate of aging in animals can be rather easily altered. The science of experimental gerontology has as its mission to find out what aging "is," and if and how its rate can be altered in man. If aging only occurred in mice or cockroaches, in the way that a special kind of aging occurs in salmon which have bred, it would not make a whole subject for study.

The idea of altering the rate of aging is an old one, going back to the alchemists. Between 1300 and 1900 it was solely the preserve of quacks. There was a flurry shortly before the turn of the century with the discovery of hormones and the attempt of the physician and physiologist Brown-Séquard to rejuvenate himself with testicle extract. But aging is not controlled by hormones, and Serge Voronoff, the physician who implanted chimpanzee testes into prosperous Europeans, produced only brass monkeys and patients who aged at the normal rate. The problem was not so much one of quackery as of timing. It is only now that biology is really ready. The background of premature attempts to control aging left its mark for many years, and it was not until the 1950s that operational attempts to alter the rate of human decline with time were seriously set afoot.

It is essential for people—who are going to be the eventual beneficiaries of gerontology research—to understand what is and what is not being researched. "Rejuvenation" is not on the agenda, in the sense of discovering a form of magic masquerading as a science by which a person already biologically old can be made biologically young. Barely enough is known about aging processes to slow them down, let alone run them backward if that were ever feasible. Nor is "prolongation of life" the key target. The Greek story tells how Tithonus married the Dawn Goddess and got her to pray to Zeus to render him immortal. Unfortunately, he forgot to ask to remain young. In consequence he was immortal but increasingly decrepit, until he prayed, as the saying now goes, to die with dignity. There is a real risk of palliative medicine producing Tithonuses by keeping people semialive and not considering the quality of their lives. Accordingly, most people, if asked, "Would you take a treatment in order to live to 120?" would reply, "Hell, no," thinking what they would be like at 120 under the present dispensation.

On the other hand, if one asks, "Would you like to take seventy years to reach the age of sixty?" the answer is likely to be different. This is in fact what is being studied at the present time, and, judging by the evidence, it is almost certainly feasible.

We do not as yet know what exactly triggers the decline in vigor which gerontologists are attempting to slow. There are four main bodily systems in which changes either do or might occur. Some of our cells divide throughout life and are constantly replaced. There is evidence that the new cells produced by an old man differ in capacity from those produced by a baby, and also that some cells are incapable of more than a limited number of divisions. These would be quite enough for an average life—nobody dies through running out of cell division—but the later models of these cells may be impaired, and some important kinds, for example in the immune system which regulates defense against infection and quality control against cancer, may actually run out. Other cells, notably those of the brain, never divide and are not replaced, but live as long as we do.

6I will never be an old man. To me, old age is always fifteen years older than I am.9

Bernard Baruch

Some of these may be lost, although statements about the loss of a hundred thousand brain cells a day have nothing to do with aging. This loss is insignificant and is probably connected with normal maintenance. Other cells in the brain, since they do not turn over, collect viruses and garbage generally and may suffer for it.

There are also the noncellular parts of the body, such as bone, and a structural material called collagen, which undergo time changes like any other material; and the blood vessels, which in man are both vulnerable and crucial. Excessive fat and cholesterol in the diet lead to furring, blockage and other adverse changes in these which are aggravated by the high pressure at which the blood system has to run.

Theories of aging are innumerable. One, that there is some general chemical-damage process which attacks both cellular and inert parts of the body, has led to the trial of chemicals, known as antioxidants, to retard aging. Antioxidants are materials which are put in such man-made structures as automobile tires to prevent perishing, and appear in the small print on labels of food to which

Golda Meir claimed to be ending almost a half-century career in politics when, in 1974, at the age of seventy-five, she resigned as Israel's Prime Minister, a post she had held for five years and through two Middle East wars. In 1976, however, she was asked to head a committee to rejuvenate the Labor Party.

Victor Hugo, French poet, playwright and novelist, published his last great work at the age of eighty-one. A lifelong republican, he had spent nineteen years in exile rather than accept the dictatorship of Louis Napoleon. After his return to France, when he was sixty-eight, already a member of the Academy and a peer of France, he was elected to the Senate. He spent his late years championing republicanism and writing voluminously.

they have been added to stop spoilage. Both perishing and spoilage, as well as the mischief done to living and nonliving materials by sunlight or gamma rays, are caused by the destructive action of free radicals. A free radical is not a member of the SLA, but is a highly active chemical moiety which has been likened to a convention delegate away from his wife—it will combine destructively with anything which is around. *If* the delicate programming and structural molecules of the body were attacked in this way with time, and *if* antioxidants slowed the process, they could possibly be used to slow aging, as they are used to slow perishing in tires, without bothering much more about where and how they act. I start with this theory, which is probably wrong, because it provides an example of the kind of tryout research on which gerontology has had to rely so far.

Antioxidants, or some of them, do slow the aging of mice. All gerontological work which involves such potentially risky trials is done upon rats or mice; their life span of two to two and a half years is less than the tenure of a Ph.D. student, and there is no alternative to them if the intention is to work with mammals. A rabbit can live ten years or more and a dog twenty years; the few experiments which have been done with dogs are lifetime studies for those who undertake them. All work on a time process has a time scale, and this has been one of gerontology's biggest problems.

The antioxidants which "slow aging" in mice, or at least make them live longer, have other actions, however. One is to upset their whole hormone economy by stimulating the liver to turn over chemicals faster. The other arises from the fact that if you feed mice a large amount of an unpleasant chemical in their diet they eat less.

The rate of aging in mammals can be easily and fundamentally changed by altering the intake of dietary calories. This remains the most important demonstration in gerontology. It was first observed in the 1930s and has still not been fully worked out, but it indicates that what is being tried in "slowing down aging" is probably not only feasible but is also relatively easily feasible without expensive technology.

The story starts with a certain Professor H. S. Osgood, at Cornell University, who believed, rightly, that humans in America eat too much. In experimenting on himself to produce pleasant satiety without food, he stretched his diet first with washed sand and later with tiny glass balls. Osgood died at the normal age. His pupil Clive McCay tried the experiment of dividing rats at weaning into two groups. One group on the normal rat diet grew up, aged and died at the rate usual for rats. The other group was kept on a diet which contained everything except sufficient calories to grow. On this spartan regime the rats remained juvenile and sexually immature—and they were still so when their siblings were entering senility. At this point McCay fed them fully. Growth restarted, and the retarded rats went through their normal life cycle about a thousand days late, thus living in the aggregate twice as long.

This slowing-by-retarding development is striking, but perhaps not surprising. Far more surprising was the observation made soon after by many researchers that no delay in development was necessary. Both the life span and the reproductive life of mice can be nearly doubled by the simple expedient of feeding them two days out

> It is day by day that we go forward; today we are as we were yesterday and tomorrow we shall be like ourselves today. So we go on without being aware of it, and this is one of the miracles of Providence that I so love.
>
> Mme. de Sevigny

of three. In this case there was no great prolongation of babyhood. The effect appears to be an overall postponement of all the senile changes which occur in mice, from coat graying to loss of reproductive power, into higher ages. Tumors in particular were postponed, some of them right out of the life cycle.

Three questions arise here. The first is, is there any chance that aging in man could be manipulated like this? The probable answer is yes, since exactly similar effects have been described in a great many organisms, from one-celled suctorians to pigs. We could be wrong, however. Mice are annuals in the wild, and may have a special slowdown mechanism which enables them to overwinter (otherwise there would be no mice). Moreover, man has a built-in slowdown in growth in normal childhood, coinciding with Sigmund Freud's "latency period." The only way to find out would be to try.

The second question is, therefore, why haven't gerontologists tried? This is a simple diet experiment, no less ethical or more tiresome than a lot of previous experiments with diet, and, in fact, bound to do some good, since, as Osgood believed, about 30 percent of Americans die basically of overeating. The reason is inherent in gerontology. So long as aging can be measured only by seeing how long people live, the only way to see if diet affects aging is to run an eighty-year experiment, longer than the working life of the investigator, and eighty-year experiments are not on.

In order to test the possibility of dietary slowing for the age process (which would give us a life span of about 120 vigorous years, if it worked as well as in rats, although this is unlikely), or, indeed, to test anything else at all which professes to "slow aging," it would be necessary to measure the rate of aging by other than actuarial, mortality-type tests. At present, mortality is the only measure of aging and, accordingly, one of the highest priorities in research is to find others, which could be used in a three- to five-year experiment.

Tests of this kind were in fact developed to see if the irradiated Japanese at Hiroshima had an accelerated rate of aging. Such tests depend upon taking a great many measures which change with age—from hair color and muscular strength to psychometric tests—and following them over a number of years. A battery of tests of this kind still needs thought and involves a number of difficulties. If such a battery could be devised, it would

Giuseppe Verdi, Italy's greatest nineteenth-century composer, wrote two of his finest operas during his eighth decade. At seventy-three he completed his magnificent *Otello*, and when he was approaching eighty, after a lifetime devoted to raising the standard of Italian tragic opera, he composed *Falstaff*, a scintillating comedy, full of life, laughter and happiness. Verdi continued working until he was eighty-four, when he completed his *Stabat Mater*, an inspired choral work. When he died three years later the poet Bioto said, ". . . he has carried away with him an enormous measure of light and vital warmth. We had all basked in the sunshine of that Olympian old age."

Benjamin Franklin, writer, scientist, inventor and one of the greatest statesmen of the American Revolution, achieved his most notable political triumphs in his later life.
At seventy, he was a member of the committee that drafted the Declaration of Independence and was one of its signers. He was seventy-five when he negotiated the peace with Great Britain. Considered "the wisest American," he was eighty-one when he effected the compromise that brought the Constitution of the United States into being.

be possible not only to compare the aging of treated and untreated groups but also to pick out and investigate persons and groups aging unusually fast or slowly, and to detect environmental influences. If eating cornflakes or using toothpaste makes us age fast, we would now have no way of knowing this.

The third question is, would Americans adopt some tiresome diet or fasting regime, even if it were shown that it doubled life span by halving the rate of aging? In view of the record of smoking and cancer, a cynic would say no, but possibly that would not be the outcome. Since 1960, most aging research has been focused on changes in cells and the chemical programs they contain. Dietary restriction, however, probably does not act directly on cells and molecules, but on some sensing mechanism in the brain which regulates the total body process. It is conceivable that this mechanism could be identified and manipulated—either by fooling it that we were eating less than we were or by altering the setting. There is even the outside possibility that some operant accessible to biofeedback and to operant conditioning could be found which could train us for slower aging, yogi-fashion. This is science fiction at present, but the fact that aging can be slowed across the board by a relatively simple maneuver is not. Accordingly, even if the mouse technique did not work in man, it at least indicates that, given the correct leverage, this kind of manipulation is feasible.

Cellular theories of aging have dealt mostly with either the entry with time of errors into the chemical blueprints stored in cells or with faulty copying on the model of prints taken from prints, which deteriorate in accuracy with the number of recopying events. It used to be thought that cells grown outside the body could divide forever, chiefly through the work of Alexis Carrel, the inventor of tissue culture, who grew chick fibroblasts in flasks. Since he used chick-embryo extract to feed them, he put more fibroblasts in at each feeding, a fact which he did not notice, although his technicians did. They were too kind or, knowing Carrel, who was a great fan of Adolf Hitler, too scared to tell him.

Recent work, particularly that of Leonard Hayflick at Stanford University, has shown that cells grown in culture outside the body are capable of only about fifty-five doublings, after which they deteriorate and "go to pieces." The exceptions, covering all the many cell strains that are propagated indefinitely in laboratories, are cells which are, as they say, transformed—they have undergone a change away from normal which makes them resemble malignant cells. There is evidence, from the comparison of cells taken from fetuses and from the old, that this "clock" is running in the body as well as outside it. Meanwhile, the work of Robin Holliday, at the National Institute of Medical Research in England, on cells at the end of their divisionary tether suggests that while, in such cells, most of the chemical machine tools known as enzymes are present, they are present in a damaged or nonworking state. The question is, whether this process is *the* aging process, that is, the process which times human deterioration with age, or only *an* aging process, the fuse of which is too long for it to time our aging.

The acid test would be to find a maneuver which prolonged the survival of such dividing cells and then show that it prolonged the life of mice and, finally, of man. Maneuvers are known which accelerate the deterioration of cells in culture—some of these throw light on what may be going on, but gerontologists rightly dislike key experiments which turn on shortening life. One can shorten the life of a mouse by hitting it over the head, but this is not accelerated aging, whereas a ten-year-old mouse would speak strongly for the theoretical manipulation which produced it.

Another wide field of research which may lead to clinical uses is concerned with the immune system. This system produces both the antibodies and the cells with which the body defends itself against infections, and the machinery which recognizes grafts or faulty cells as "not self" and rejects them. Immunological disorder does, indeed, produce a vague and generalized disorganization very like that seen in aging. On the basis that there may be faulty copying of cells with age, it has been theorized that it may be that cells are produced which the body treats as "not self," or that immune cells are produced which are rogues and attack normal body constituents. Recent graft research has produced powerful agents to suppress immune reactions. These do prevent the appearance of some pathologies seen in aging, but, unfortunately, they also kill the body's capacity to recognize and squelch cancer cells (most of which we probably destroy before they do mischief). The work of Takashi Makinodan, who put old immune cells into young mice and young immune cells into old mice, has shown that both the cells concerned and the body as a whole lose immunologic efficiency with age. He has also found that some clinically important manipulations are possible. It may be that what is needed is to boost or to resharpen immune reaction so that censorship of mismade cells becomes stricter. Both cancer research (which is attempting to find immune ways of getting the body to kill cancer cells) and aging research (which is concerned about mismade cells in general) are attempting to find useful forms of interference here.

Hormones, the old standby of physiologists in the 1900s, when hormones meant sex hormones and rejuvenation meant sexual rejuvenation, have clinical uses in treating aging, especially in women, when hormone supplementation after the menopause has good cosmetic

effects and prevents the condition of the bones which leads to stooping and deformity in late old age. But there is no one hormone which controls the aging process in general. Women—and all female mammals—tend to live longer than males. This may be due to long-term effects of the male-hormone economy, especially on blood vessels, since eunuchs outlive entire males, or to the male's pair of unlike chromosomes, which lays him open

Cicely Courtneidge and Jack Hulbert celebrated their diamond wedding anniversary in 1976 when he was eighty-four and she was eighty-three. Household names in Britain during the thirties, forties and fifties, when they starred, often together, in numerous plays, revues and films, they never lost their love of the theater or their desire to work. In 1970 they toured South Africa and then returned to Britain where, on a hectic schedule, they continued to make guest appearances and to appear in plays all over the country.

to the effects of an adverse gene on either one of them, since there is no second copy to "cover" it. It may be even that, being programmed to live with a half-foreign fetus, women stand up better to immunologic aging than do men. Darwin called this "feminine advantage" a natural process due to sex alone—in other words, he did not know why it happens, and nor do we. If chromosomes are involved, then the position should be reversed in birds, where the female has the unlike chromosomes, and there is a little evidence in favor of this theory.

The atom bomb, and experiments indicating that radiation exposure appears to accelerate aging, gave rise to a long period of mutation-based theories, starting from the idea that the information store in some or all cells becomes damaged with time. This idea is not now widely popular, because drugs which gravely damage cell information do not always affect life span. Recently, interest has moved back from the cell, the double helix and cellular information, to general physiology—in particular to an old idea, that there may be an aging "clock" in the brain. There is, apparently, a clock of this kind which triggers puberty and, interestingly enough, it is coupled to the attainment of a particular body weight. Even immune processes are under brain control.

In mice, there seems to be a similar clock which terminates reproductive life, and this one can be restarted by the substance L-dopa, used in treating parkinsonism. L-dopa is one of a number of important chemicals known as catecholamines. (Amphetamines belong to this group.) Those which occur naturally in the brain are implicated both in clock-type processes and in maintaining normal mood—when depression or excitement occurs, it often is cyclical. With aging, the chemical composition of some brain areas tends to drift in a direction characteristic of depression. This may be because old age in America is depressing, but it may equally be built in, and explain why antidepressants, like procraine, make old folk feel better. (See *KH3*.)

There is much more which could be said about gerontological research. Probably the facts which the ordinary citizen most needs to know are these: (1) The exact nature of "aging" and whether it is one process or many, are unknown but are under intensive study. (2) The rate of aging has been shown to be alterable en bloc, so that all age diseases occur later. (3) Very probably the rate of aging could be altered in man. (4) How soon we known whether and how it can be done depends solely upon our social investment in doing it.

In 1974 Congress voted a National Institute of Aging Studies, destined to be the NASA of this type of investigation. The price tag on a fundamental slowing of aging in man is, on a reasonable guesstimate, one-fifth the Soyuz space circus plus some time. It might fail (so might the Moon landing have done), but it probably will not. What we need to decide is whether we want it.

Gerontology will not abolish old age; it will make it happen later. If it lengthens life, it will temporarily increase the population, but as world population is already

Henrik Ibsen, the great nineteenth-century Norwegian playwright, dramatically changed his style of writing when he was in his sixties. These later plays are generally considered his finest and most imaginative. A relentless worker, it was his practice to devote two years to a single play, working from copious notes which he constantly revised. He completed *The Master Builder* when he was sixty-four and *John Gabriel Borkman* when he was sixty-eight. His brilliant final work, *When We Dead Awake*, was written four years later.

doubling every thirty-three years, its worldwide effect will be negligible. The extra years, unless we persist in clock-watching in defiance of all reason, will be years of extra vigor, not dependency. Old age itself will not be longer, only later—say from eighty to ninety instead of seventy to eighty. A treated man or woman of seventy will have precisely the physical condition and disabilities he or she would have had at sixty, plus more time to learn. With even greater retardation, if that proved possible, we would tend to become elephants (long life, slow turnover) rather than mice (short life, high turnover) with all that that implies. Attention must be devoted to the social effects of what is now a contingency before it becomes an option.

How far, in addition to this rate-based approach, particular age disabilities will be removable depends in sum upon what is learned, and what aging itself proves to be. Aldous Huxley's fantasy of seventy years of cosmetic youth followed by sudden death, without any decline, is unlikely and a little inhuman. More can be done to palliate age now by altering our attitudes to it, which cause most of its miseries, than by drugs or manipulations, although these have a place. Of the known agents affecting aging, the caloric-restriction experiments, much extended in the work of Dr. Morris Ross at Fox Springs, offer the best lead for human work, and human work is what we need—who needs old mice? By working on man directly we become open to serendipity, we are working on our intended beneficiary and any gain is an immediate gain.

There is presently no pill, remedy, vitamin, diet or other gimmick recommendable to delay aging. All commercially promoted nostra of this kind without exception are fraudulent (see *Quackery*)—this follows from the fact that there is no way yet in which they could be tested. Dietary means might control human aging, but the diets used in past experimentation have been designed for rodents, and mere starvation does not prolong life, it shortens it. (For details of sensible diet in age, see *Food*.) If you ask what you should take to have a chance of delaying your own aging, the answer is, "Take the trouble to write to your congressman and to get the National Institute of Aging Studies as generously funded as one paranoiac weapon or one South American dictator." The control of the human rate of aging is going to happen. How soon it happens, and whether you

6 To be seventy years young is sometimes far more cheerful and hopeful than to be forty years old. 9

Oliver Wendell Holmes

yourself are Joshua or only Moses, depends upon the social pressure for research and the wisdom with which that research is applied.

Hair. Graying of hair is the best-known age change. It depends apparently upon actual loss of pigment cells, so it cannot be biologically reversed. Its timing is genetic: white horses are born black, but whiten within a year; gorillas gray at maturity; some humans have genetically gray forelocks, while others gray early in life in some hairs, but not in others—the process known as roaning, which is imitated in certain fashionable hairstyles.

If you don't like gray hair on yourself you need not have it, given modern hairdressing technology, provided that your skin tolerates hair dyes. Remember that during any period of illness or inability to go out, hair color grows out at the roots, and the cosmetic effect is then worse than leaving well enough alone.

The texture of hair in both sexes changes with age (in women, hormone supplements slow this change after the menopause when it is marked). Late in life it's a good idea to aim at a trouble-free hairstyle so that you don't have to travel to maintain it. At the same time, going out in the interest of keeping yourself in good and attractive shape is valuable, provided you are not actually sick or infirm. Long hair can be a nuisance if you are stiff, as you can't easily reach to comb it. Loss of hair is rare in women, except in thyroid deficiency. In men, baldness is genetic, occurs in early or late maturity and can't be prevented or slowed by any of the routines promoted to delay it. You can get hair transplanted into your scalp at vast expense, making the top of your head look a little like a neglected orange plantation, but the transplants rarely last long. There seems little point—any more than if a silverback gorilla dyed himself to look juvenile.

Wigs are good now and save trouble in hairdressing, but you need one which looks like your natural hair, for you have to face yourself every time you take it off.

Hearing is one area in which age changes are universal or nearly so. These changes start around age thirty. The universal change is a falloff in the ability to hear high-pitched notes, but this varies a lot in different individuals and it is only disabling when extreme. With time, other ear problems can accumulate. At very high ages there can be hearing loss, about equal in both ears, with very little obvious cause.

Hearing, therefore, is vulnerable. It is also highly important. Deafness interferes with all sorts of social interaction, especially at a time when society is trying to isolate you and ease you out. It used to be said that the cheapest hearing aid is a piece of string; put one end in your ear and the other in your breast pocket, and everyone yells like a fiend. If you are statutorily "old," however, they don't bother, or they yell unhelpfully. Just how much deafness can do to shut you down is indicated by the fact that in old age it correlates highly with paranoia —pathological suspicion of what others are up to that you can't hear. The suspicion is often justified.

While 5 percent of people have hearing difficulties at fifty, some 27 percent have them over age seventy-four and about 11 percent complain, as Beethoven did, of distracting noise in the ears. You may also find that you "take in" information a little more slowly (there seems to be a decline in channel capacity).

This is an area in which you have to take active steps. So long as you think deafness is a natural penalty of age you may not take them. In a British survey, half the moderately deaf older folk had stayed away from the doctor for this reason, thinking nothing could be done. In an American study, 34 percent of deaf older people had never had a hearing test and only 18 percent had had one in the previous two years.

Even in Britain, where hearing aids are available without charge on prescription, only 400,000 out of 1,300,000 deaf people over sixty-five have them. Either they regard deafness as a natural part of aging or they aren't aware that treatment is possible, and the same appears to be true of some doctors.

The strategy for avoiding or dealing with hearing difficulty is simple but important. It consists of (1) regular checkups—so that you don't wait until what is usually a gradual loss impairs functioning; (2) active treatment of any treatable disease in a hospital ear department, exactly as you would get at a younger age; (3) a proper, working hearing aid. This should only be got after consultation with an otologist, as hearing aids are a favorite swindle pitch (see *Rip-offs*). You may not need one or it may make your speech comprehension worse.

6 Old wood is best to burn,
old wine to drink,
old friends to trust,
and old authors to read. . . . 9

Anon.

The final fallback, in the unlikely event that you become severely and untreatably deaf, is to learn to lip-read as younger deaf people do. More often what is needed is some assertion training. It's easy to lapse out of conversation because people are impatient with your apparent dullness and stupidity, but if you give in you have had it. Tell them repeatedly, "I want to hear all your pearls of wisdom. Will you kindly speak slowly, facing me, without a cigar in your jaw, turn off the Muzak and stop shouting? If you don't, I'll assume you don't want me to hear or are not saying anything worth hearing."

Don't go back to any doctor you consult about this who starts with "Well, of course" and then mentions your chronological age. Noise, incidentally, damages hearing. This is what used to happen to boilermakers. There are going to be some very deaf rock guitarists come A.D. 2000.

Hobbies are fine if you like them and if they express your identity. But a hobby is no good as a substitute for engaged living. On the other hand, a hobby of your first trajectory can become an earning occupation for your second, and as retirement approaches it is worth scrutinizing hobby skills.

We haven't gone deeply into hobbies here. We prefer occupation.

Hypothermia. In old age King David "gat him no heat." This is a general trend with aging. Accordingly, older people in cold places need fuel. Very many senior deaths in Britain (among old people with inadequate funds to buy fuel or who are unable to carry coal or who have the toilet at the bottom of the garden) are due to cold. Others try to get warm with makeshift heating equipment and die in fires (see Fire). This seems to be less of a problem in America, because the severer midwestern and northern climates are reflected in house design.

Influenza is one of the infectious diseases which can kill far more easily in later life than in early life. Regular immunization against it is a lifesaving or health-saving measure for older people.

Charles de Gaulle was sixty-eight years old when, in 1958, he was returned to power and acknowledged as the only man who could avert civil war in France while giving Algeria independence. He remained President of France until 1969, when he returned to private life. He continued to write his memoirs until his death at the age of eighty.

Intelligence is what mathematicians call a "fuzzy" character, but whatever it is, folklore, incorporated into a great many textbooks, indicates that it "declines with age"—from age twenty-six on, according to Wechsler, who invented some of the standard intelligence tests.

Intelligence tests don't in fact measure what we ordinarily mean by intelligence, namely mental brightness and ability. Most of them measure the ability to do

Charles Darwin, the famous English naturalist, produced many scientific achievements in later life, in spite of much public opposition and intermittent bouts of ill-health. A man of enormous tenacity, he worked methodically. As follow-ups to his *On the Origin of Species*, which appeared in 1859, when he was fifty, he completed *The Descent of Man* at the age of sixty-two and *The Expression of the Emotions in Man and Animals* the very next year. After a heart attack in 1873, he persisted in his work and produced, among several other books, *The Power of Movement in Plants* at seventy-one.

intelligence tests, in conformity with the expectations of white, middle-class schoolteachers. In studies, older people sometimes have done poorly on these tests. They were brought up in a competitive society, they know that the old are supposed to be stupid and they move to the defensive.

Carl Eisdorfer, who has been a leader in unscrambling nonsense over age and intelligence, points out that a lot of the tests used for older people are kids' tests, with an aura about them of school or examinations; accordingly, the test material is seen by older people as dull, pointless or silly. They suspect that they are being childrenized. Even more to the point, while kids are tested to death, older people haven't taken an examination in years, if at all, and they are pardonably suspicious—and they also know that they are supposed to be failing. It's a bit like being asked to have sex in public when you've been told you are probably impotent. It doesn't help.

Previous researchers were misled by looking cross-sectionally at age groups whose educational experience was different, rather than following single individuals over the years. Several studies show that even given classroom-type tests, there is virtually no sign of decline in the intelligence of normal, healthy individuals past sixty. What does decline is speed—with increasing age people rush themselves less and respond badly to being rushed by others. The one exception, noted in studies which followed the same individuals for many years, was in people with untreated high blood pressure. This is an illness and probably damages brain function. Exclude these individuals, and any who have other active diseases of the brain or its blood supply, and the "decline" in mental capacity is insignificant. In Eisdorfer's words, "The notion that adults, by virtue of arriving at a certain age, such as sixty-five, all fall off the edge and become senile and incompetent is both ludicrous and frightening. It is frightening because, like any other group that bears the weight of discrimination and deprivation, the older group accepts for itself the evaluation put on it by society."

What really happens in psychological aging is complex and still unclear. One fact is that the variation in nearly all attributes goes up. We all know that some people of eighty are demented because of illness while others conduct orchestras. The reason so little is known is that we haven't paid to find out. Society (our society, that is) treats people like armaments. We spend the early years testing and loading them. At the end of their education we fire them, and the going word is that they then pursue a downward trajectory by their own proper motion. They become what Eisdorfer calls "superfluous people . . . for whom we have no use and about whom we have very little information, so we act as if they did not exist and mediate resources to them as if they did not exist."

As with intelligence, so with learning. Conscious of what amounts to a hostile audience and themselves indoctrinated with their own declining ability, older people relieve their anxiety in any paced learning task by taking it more slowly and carefully. In an Australian experiment, a class of seventy-year-olds, without being specially motivated, learned German, using the same books and classrooms, at exactly the same rate and with the same passing grades as fifteen-year-olds. Present-day oldsters in America are in gross a less educated group than their successors will be. And ten years ago, among *their* predecessors, there were about a million functional illiterates. The upcoming old, therefore, have not only the ability to learn, but also have more training in the skills of doing so.

In some ways, aging helps with learning because it involves experience, and experience helps us to organize input. By sixty, if we use our minds at all, our filing system and our vocabulary are pretty strong. We no longer take in information as single pieces, but as additions to a "block," much as it gets easier to run an office when there is a file on each topic, rather than a lot of sheets of paper laid out singly.

One finding in some studies is that older people avoid risk-taking behavior in decision making. Part of this is due to the wiliness of experience, and part to self-defense. They have plenty to lose in a culture which believes that older folk are inept and will fail. Although perfectly able to learn, in a learning situation older people get upset and anxious because of fear of failure. They may in fact appear not to learn because they would rather risk not answering than to give a wrong answer which confirms their own fears and other people's prejudices. They are in the position of the only black pupil in a class of hostile whites where the teacher prefaces a text by expressing the view that black people are naturally stupid. A very tough character might be moved by anger to

'Ah, nothing is too late,
'Til the tired heart shall
   cease to palpitate.
Cato learned Greek at eighty;
   Sophocles
Wrote his grand Oedipus, and
   Simonides
Bore off the prize of verse
   from his compeers
When each had numbered
   more than fourscore years.'

Henry Wadsworth Longfellow

120

Marie Stopes, the pioneer of
the British birth control
movement, was an able scientist
whose ability was matched by
her courage. She opened
Britain's first birth control
clinic in 1921 when she was
forty-one. For years, hers
was a single-minded, almost
single-handed battle against
opposition and general
suspicion. But she remained
active in the running of her
clinic and for twenty-two years,
until her death in 1958, at the
age of seventy-eight, she
worked indefatigably to
promote birth control in Asia.

excel and teach the bastards a lesson. The history of European anti-Semitism shows that persecution and hostility can be a spur to achievement, although it is the kind of spur that few people feel they need. For the older person, however, the pressure isn't overt enough to get him or her sufficiently mad to respond in this way. And the most destructive part of it is built in, through having grown up "knowing" that older people can't perform.

A Martian anthropologist, studying the inhabitants of Earth, wouldn't see the aging American as a spent carcass pushed out by the more able young whose initiative and intelligence have been unimpaired by built-in obsolescence. He would start by noting the middle-class Western obsession with success, youth, push and competition. He would observe how, as the hands of the clock point to the time when tradition decrees we get a gold watch and the boot, we start looking around like the Roman priest of Nemi, who constantly watched for the successor who would kill him and take his place.

A society generates garbage attitudes and garbage science to justify garbage policies. The policy of "expendable people" is one of these and much pseudo-scientific writing is part of the circular process of maintaining this policy. At the moment the age level for unpersonhood is coming down. (This is called early retirement.) Just as soon as forty- or thirty-year-olds become expendable people, papers on their psychological deficiencies will start to appear, folklore will be adjusted and people will themselves start to believe that at forty or at thirty, they are "past it." Or else, assisted in growing a backbone by the increasing militancy of those in the long-penalized age groups, they will start kicking. One hopes for the second alternative.

KH3 is the "Rumanian miracle drug" which is discussed as a remedy for aging, or at least as an improver for the old.

There are two laws in respect to rejuvenatory and similar drugs. The first is that miracle drugs, vitamins, treatments and others in like case offending are excellent for rejuvenating their proprietors' bank accounts. The second is that anything very expensive and not available from a straight geriatric clinic is a rip-off.

KH3—or, rather its cheap and widely available active ingredient, the dental anesthetic procaine (the injection which makes your jaw go numb)—differs from other publicized medications for use in age because there is possibly something in it, although not what the Rumanian team who promoted it thought.

Procaine is usually injected into tissues or close to nerves as a local anesthetic. Many years ago workers in England tried to relieve arthritic pain by injecting procaine into a blood vessel, and noted that it had some general effects (in making patients "feel better," and in mimicking the effects of the hormone which turns on the adrenal cortex). Anna Aslan, a Rumanian doctor, found similar effects. She gave it to elderly people and made them "feel much better." Dr. Aslan, however, is a charismatic lady, who took good care of her patients, listened to what they said and combined her doses of procaine with what we should call good supportive geriatrics and psychotherapy. The question, then, was— which did the trick, the shots or the milieu?

Professor Chebotarev of the Kiev Institute of Gerontology in the Soviet Union and doctors in the United States tested procaine. The American studies suggested, although not conclusively, that the Rumanian-made procaine influenced well-being. The Russians tried the Aslan preparation on more than one thousand older people. No physical benefit was observed, in terms of present disease or reversal of age changes, but most takers felt significantly better. A few had side effects and had to be taken off it.

It is difficult to test procaine "double-blind," as the injection feels different from that of saline or an inactive solution. Most tests suggest that it can improve mood. Noting this, researchers looked back at an old finding that procaine belongs to a group of substances known as MAO inhibitors, which are effective in the treatment of depression. Most of these are risky or tiresome to use, because they render the body unable to deal with normal constituents of dietary staples like cheese or red wine, so that these become effectively poisonous as long as the drug is taken. This is not the case with procaine. Consequently, the Federal Drug Administration has authorized trials, now in progress, to see if Anna Aslan's geriatric discovery provides a safe mood elevator for use in later life. Procaine is a substance with a number of actions, and it might conceivably influence age processes in other ways, but there is no evidence of this, nor is it a "vitamin," "hormone" or, so far as we know, anything but a mood elevator. In old mice, MAO drugs such as pro-

6 Youth is happy because it has the ability to see beauty. Anyone who keeps the ability to see beauty never grows old.9

Franz Kafka

caine do appear able to restart ovulation when it ceases, but there is no evidence of such action in people.

Mood improvement in itself would be useful. Depressions, often so mild we don't notice them for what they are, are one of the main enemies of later life—not only because society often makes age a depressing business, but also because it appears that with aging the chemistry of the brain tilts in a direction which may be conducive to depression.

Procaine isn't available in normal practice as an antidepressant, but it is an everyday drug with few serious risks. If you are sold on trying it you could ask your physician. Procaine itself is cheap—one dollar would be plenty for the medication itself, although if you want it injected (there is not much good evidence that it works by mouth) you'd have to pay for having the shot. A sensible line would be to wait until the research tests are finished. (See *Medication*.)

Leisure is a con. It should mean time when you do what you yourself want to do. It gets sold, as part of the unperson package, as time in which you are expected to do trivial things for which you have to pay money. People subjected to underpaid drudgery need the first sort of leisure, like the cleaning woman in nineteenth-century England who chose as her epitaph:

> *Don't weep for me now, friends,*
> *Don't weep for me never—*
> *I'm going to do nothing*
> *for ever and ever.*

But even she would have got tired of leisure after a week's paid holiday.

People only need leisure if they do dull, resented or exploited work, and even then they don't need the Coney Island–Retirement Village package which makes them into permanent children; this is good for an afternoon, not for a life-style. What the retired need, what the unemployed need and what more and more of us shall need as commercial rationalization pushes us out of participant living, isn't "leisure," it's occupation. Leisure supplied as a package is something to chuck right back at the suppliers, unless you want to buy the whole phony aging package along with it. Get occupation first. Leisure in the right sense will follow, if you find you have time for it.

Edward Kennedy "Duke" Ellington never retired from anything except booze—which he gave up when he was in his mid-forties. For almost half a century he kept his band together, always on the road or circling the globe. He made his first recording in 1924 and his last in 1974, not many weeks before his death at the age of seventy-five. He left a great legacy—the most distinctive single body of composition in the history of jazz.

Lights. Two inevitabilities with the passage of time are decreased visual acuity and increased bone brittleness. Accordingly, one important piece of self-defense, which can put years on to your active life, is to avoid falling down (see *Falls*). One of the best ways of doing this is to go through the house or apartment looking for two kinds of booby trap—unlit areas with stairs, carpet edges or other pitfalls and areas where a combination of lighting, pattern and edges could make you misjudge your step. Having found these, either alter them or, in the case of dark spots on a main thoroughfare, get them properly lit. Don't, if you can help it, do this with portable lamps. These have line cords which are themselves trip wires. Also, if you plug in a Christmas tree of additional wiring to an outlet, you can blow the circuit or set a fire.

Not everyone loses sight with age, although most people need glasses. The commonest problem, which proper lighting can help, is cataract. (See *Sight*.) Samuel Pepys used to read with two paper tubes fixed to his spectacle frames to cut out cross-lighting, which illuminates the opacity in the eye, not the page. Try reading with a spotlight on your book from over your shoulder, with the room lights turned off.

Living in Sin is a highly satisfactory solution, at any age, to loneliness and is in favor of sexuality and mutual support if marriage penalizes you financially or if you prefer it. Neither the state nor the neighbors nor your children have any right to demand that you take out a marriage license. But remember that in the event of sudden widowhood, wives are entitled to security advantages, at least in community-property states.

Loneliness versus Being Alone. Loneliness is being alone when you don't want that. A great deal is written about the loneliness of old age, and some people do indeed complain bitterly of abandonment. At the same time, 80 percent of people over sixty-five live with someone else, and 86 percent, according to one study, had seen a relative in the preceding week.

Probably the first point to remember is that cities produce, or contain, lonely people of all ages—including teenagers. It's factually doubtful whether loneliness is really commoner in later life than it is in early and middle life, except for two factors. The first of these is bereavement. A lot of people who are lonely in later life are actually bereaved—often after very long associations with the dead person. It's harder, given the meaning we place on aging, to get over this than it might have been earlier on, and when outlets like work activity, which could lighten mourning, have been sealed off. American women, who often marry older men but are inherently likely to live longer than males, have about a 70 percent expectation of widowhood, but in a culture which can't deal well with death at any age, they rarely rehearse how they will handle this likely outcome. Close to the probable end of one's own life, too, it seems too great an effort to "get over" bereavement; as the saying goes, it's hardly worth going home. (See *Bereavement*.)

The other prime cause of loneliness is illness. Most old people who say they are lonely are in fact ill—some psychologically, others physically. Illness saps mobility and loosens the grip on life and may make us drop contacts and friendships. And this is a vicious circle.

We're not saying that loneliness is not a problem in age, only that it's not confined to the last part of life and that it then commonly has components of bereavement and of illness—including under that heading the increasing embitterment some people feel because of the treatment they've had from life, from society and from themselves. This isn't devalued by inclusion as "illness." The point is that it makes them ill, justified as their feelings may have been.

Most old people who are not ill, whether bereaved or not, do manage to handle loneliness at least as well as younger age groups by dealing with it through their own resources. One enormous reservoir of unhappiness could be drained if we expected older people to work and allowed them to do so. Work, unless it's wholly solitary, is the natural antidote to loneliness.

After work, the next layer of resource (if we insist on keeping over sixty-fives as a segregated group) is the development of senior centers, where something more is available than keep-fit and knitting classes— preferably community organization in favor of senior rights. This would be much better, of course, as a people center, without meaningless age limits, rather than a senior center, but it has to start somewhere (see *Day Centers*) and could combine communal dining with educational and activist activities and an employment organization and an advice bureau.

> That he was never less at leisure than when at leisure; nor that he was ever less alone than when alone.

Cicero

Last of all, there is a minority who don't, won't or can't go out, and who need a find-and-visit operation by a volunteer flying squad operating out of the "senior center." Some people, as at all ages, won't be "helpable," but the majority will welcome such attention pathetically. (Maybe they only have stairs they dare not negotiate.) They can regain their sense of self. The turnaround produced by a little community concern can be amazing, although we wouldn't be so amazed if we thought and felt a little.

If you are lonely but can walk, go and get some such operation going, even if it's on a one-man or a one-woman scale to start with. You will find it helps others and cures you.

Love is a multipurpose word—we "love" our spouse, child, country, parents, Beethoven, skiing, all in different senses. The commonest modern context is sexual, and that type of love is lifelong (see *Sex*). Both this and the other meanings are especially important as age advances. One thing they have in common is engagement, and it is this capacity which most preserves us. If at eighty we can "love" in any of the disparate senses of that word, that implies that there is something or somebody with which or whom we retain human engagement; It is best if the object is a person, but of some value still if we can "love" music, reading or a particular place. The real psychologic unity of "loving" is the retention of an outgoing sense of our own identity, able to lay hold on experience and on the experience of another person. It probably takes the assaults of time to make us truly value this capacity. Old people are therefore either loving people or tragic people who have outlived the quality of engagement. This is why compulsory exclusion and the impoverishment of daily experience which we often impose on the old are so profoundly damaging to them.

Masturbation used to be a major focus of medico-moral hogwash. It is now recognized as "a normal and healthy act for any person of either sex and at any age"—part of the human biosexual program, in fact. Its uses change during life: in preadolescence and adolescence masturbation is our commonest way into sexual sensation (in our culture, at least); then it becomes a form of sexual exercise which improves female response and male staying power and develops fantasy; in adult married life it is part of love play and a source of variety in sensation; in later life masturbation serves not only as a fill-in for those without partners or a gentler source of orgasm for the infirm, but also as maintenance, as well as a sexual outlet, to bridge any periods of nonintercourse. This is especially important in the male, who may otherwise find it hard to restart (see *Sex*).

Manual stimulation gets built into intercourse with increasing age because older males need it to get firm erection, so don't be self-conscious about handwork on each other. Since older men also commonly get one orgasm in two or three acts of intercourse, you have a choice—either you or your partner can terminate any act manually. But if you do this every time, you will get far fewer coital orgasms since you will push up the firing threshold.

Women who have learned to masturbate add it to their sexual repertoire and will use it throughout life when they wish. Nobody wishes to "push" sexual activity on people it doesn't suit, and who would take that as an impertinence, but it's worth mentioning that it's never too late to buy stock in your own sexuality.

Women of seventy and eighty who had never had an orgasm have learned to masturbate for the first time, with or without a modern vibrator, some on the promptings of turned-on daughters, others from following the advice of a counseling clinic; they went to the clinic because they didn't want to die without that part of the experience of womanhood. We should view masturbation in later life like this, not as a reversion to the baby's use of it as a comforter, suitable for old, rejected, sexually spent people in second childhood. As in adolescence, because our culture used to prohibit it and still feels a little self-conscious about it, masturbation is a healthy gesture of life-affirming defiance—one source of sexual pleasure that the rejecting and the antisexual can't stop you having.

Now that sexology has a better idea of the function and uses of masturbation at different ages, people are learning to make intelligent use of it as a sexual enhancer and adjustment. If you learned it guiltily in childhood, and were in two minds about it as an adult, you need to re-examine it, and your own body, leisurely, now. Masturbation is not in any way a substitute for sexual partnership, but it's a supplement, of equal value to men and to women.

Josephine Baker, the St. Louis
girl who was adopted by the
French as their own, returned
to the United States in 1973,
when she was sixty-six, to give
four concerts in Carnegie Hall.
Wearing a spangled body
stocking and a towering
headdress, she was sensational.
In 1975, shortly before her
death, she starred in an
elaborate show in Paris which
marked the fiftieth anniversary
of her debut.

Media. The media at the moment take precious little notice of the senior citizen, but demography indicates that they will very soon have to. The media are important to the old, since age reduces mobility without reducing the need to stay in touch with events. Most older people read papers or watch television, and even those who have problems reading can listen to the radio.

The media could work for the older citizen in four ways. They can combat isolation, give information about specific services and activities and, preeminently, act as a channel for continuing education in the home. They can also greatly influence attitudes, both by showing the old what age could be, and by disabusing the community at large about what age is.

The Gerontological Society is compiling a comprehensive bibliography of the material which has been made by, for and about age. Entertainment programs like *The Love Nest* have started showing the old as feisty, energetic folk setting about their own self-defense. The advent of the young-old is bound to hasten this. Not all, or even many, of the movies of the year 2000 will be about young lovers or young exploits. There will be more about older lovers and older exploits, in which older people are treated realistically as black people are now (sometimes) treated realistically. There will also be old-exploitation shows, no doubt, as there are black-exploitation shows.

With the coming of cable television, with its potential for community TV and talkback, the "company" provided now by the soap opera could become the real company of real people, and provide a reentry for the senior world into the community generally.

The media are on the other end of your telephone—use it. Protest programs which ignore you or misrepresent you, and pester for the meeting of your needs—by challenging license renewal if necessary, and, in any case, by speaking up. The programmers aren't mind readers, and will respond to organized pressure by reconsidering policies, at least in regard to low-earning, off-peak programs. Remember the use of the media in handling rip-offs and the denial of your rights. Most radio and television stations now have an action line which works wonders on public officials and slow payers and local tradesmen who sell you defective goods. If you are hassled or threatened with eviction, at least try to ensure that the press and television know about it. If

Maurice Chevalier, the famous French entertainer, was presented with a Special Academy Award in 1958 to celebrate his fifty remarkable years in show business. Then seventy years old, he by no means considered this the culmination of his career. That same year he starred in the motion picture *Gigi*, two years later enthralled a following of millions in *Can-Can* and then, when he was seventy-three, in *Fanny*.

they cover it they powerfully concentrate the mind of whoever is responsible.

One national show which represents older Americans keeping their end up and fighting put-downs, and one national magazine program by and for seniors, could achieve more in less time than a constitutional amendment asserting the right to be decently treated as you get older. You could start pressing for them now. The addresses and telephone numbers of your local network stations are in the Yellow Pages.

133

Medication. Medicines can be a boon in later life, since this is a time when physical systems often require adjustment. They can also be a menace, because it is a time when physical systems are easily put out of kilter and, in the absence of proper geriatrics teaching, few doctors have had specific training in the pharmaceutical responses of "the old." A hundred years ago, medicine leaned heavily on placebos—medicines made of plants and the like which had mild or no actions, but which expressed the doctor's concern for the patient while he or she got naturally better. The trouble is that now, instead of placebos, doctors often give highly active drugs with side effects which can play hell in their own right if they are not carefully regarded. Moreover, since complaints tend to multiply with time, older people may get not one or two, but dozens of medicines, some recently discovered, others incompatible, in a scientific attempt to cover all bases.

The first thing a geriatrician does with a patient who is confused, out of his or her head or sick with unexplained symptoms, is to review all the medication and self-medication the patient is having and to stop most of it. (For a typical example of the kind of thing geriatricians observe, see *Vitamins*.) Only too often at high ages the sequence is: mild, silent infection, mild confusion, diagnosis of "senility," tranquilizer, worse confusion, more tranquilizer, patient goes up the wall and is hospitalized, drug stopped, infection treated, patient returns to normal. This story has been given a happy ending. Most "senility" in custodial homes is aggravated by tranquilizers in the same way as insanity in mental hospitals used to be protracted by bromide poisoning. Goofballs cost less than care, and many of these preparations are advertised as making patients docile, manageable or quiet.

Older patients should not despise medication or second-guess the doctor. On the other hand, they should take no pill without a cause, and preferably then only on the prescription of a doctor who has shown his awareness of geriatric medicine by considering life-style as well as symptomatology. Often he may adopt the sound strategy of not medicating things which will get better anyway—which is wholly different from the nonstrategy of regarding discomforts in old age as inevitable.

Drugs, in sum, are a boon when properly used in old age and a menace when overused or ignorantly used.

And of these drugs, tranquilizers, sleeping pills and the manipulative medications generally are the most hazardous—they often substitute for real help, and they tend to impair such attributes as orientation and memory, which are more vulnerable in age than in youth. In particular the normal pattern of sleep in age—light nighttime sleep and the occasional daytime nap—doesn't call for sleeping pills. Antibiotics, by contrast, can be lifesavers. What is needed besides patient education is the steady building up of later-life medicine as a major speciality.

Memory. You don't, unless you're sick, run out of memory with age. What happens is that input and recall both slow down. In other words, the index file doesn't age, but the secretary is older and takes longer to put new cards in or to bring cards you want. Most people in their late fifties notice that they can't instantly recall names, for example, which are familiar but are not in constant use, as quickly and reliably as they did. These names haven't gone—they usually bob up after an hour or more, but it is awkward if you needed them there and then. This effect doesn't normally get any worse as you age further. In most cases, let the gap go—brain cudgeling can't force recall and may actually stall it. For cases where it matters, there are such memory-jogging techniques as going through the alphabet until you strike a letter which "rings a bell," then going through vowels until you get a syllable—but in most cases the name comes automatically if you leave it.

By far the best way of actually improving memory and all other mental performances is to use them—by continued activity and learning and by "enrichment of the environment." Mental deterioration would occur at any age if we had only a chair and a television set.

Bad loss of recall and embarrassing loss of memory for recent events—which are not induced by worrying *about* your memory—can be produced by illness, including untreated high blood pressure, brain artery diseases, "senile" brain damage, some drugs (especially certain kinds of sleeping pill) and alcohol. They are not features of healthy aging. The concentration of many old people on the past is chiefly a result of their current experience and put-downs in the near-at-hand scene. The past felt better, so they concentrate on it. That need not be; the present can be improved.

6There is a wicked inclination in most people to suppose an old man decayed in his intellect. If a young or middle-aged man, when leaving a company, does not recollect where he laid his hat, it is nothing; but if the same inattention is discovered in an old man, people will shrug their shoulders and say "His memory is going."9

Samuel Johnson

Artur Rubinstein was eighty-nine years old when he gave one of the most remarkable recitals in the history of New York's Carnegie Hall. As the result of a serious eye condition he could no longer see well enough to read a note of music or see the piano keys beneath his fingers, yet, relying entirely on his memory, he played better than he had ever played before.

Menopause. At the menopause two things happen. You stop ovulating and producing hormonal cycles and the pituitary gland, which used to drive these, locks in the "on" position so that your gonadotrophin level remains high. Gonadotrophins are the control hormones which "turn on" the ovaries. After this you cannot get pregnant and you will cease to menstruate. You do not become "neuter," your sex life does not end. Much more often it really begins in earnest, unhampered by contraception. The transient changes, part hormonal, part psychological, such as hot flashes, can be controlled by hormone supplements: you can even if you like be kept menstruating, although this isn't necessary and might mask uterine cancer if you get it. The late effects of the menopause, such as vaginal dryness, skin changes and bone loss make supplementation desirable in many doctors' view.

The menopause dramatizes the start of Part Two of your life. Whether or not it upsets you will depend upon how you feel about it, and how far you have been indoctrinated with a phony idea of youth and its relation to being lovable and being yourself. There is nothing in the menopause in itself, once the hormone swings settle, to make you ill. In the words of John Fothergill, the old Quaker doctor, writing during the eighteenth century, "There is a period in the life of females to which, for the most part, they are taught to look forward with some degree of anxiety. The various and absurd opinions relative to the ceasing of the menstrual discharge, propagated through successive ages, have tended to embitter the hours of many a sensible woman. Some practitioners in other respects able and judicious, if they have not favored these erroneous and terrifying notions, seem not to have endeavored to correct them with the diligence and humanity which such an object requires."

The menopause doesn't reverse itself. If later you "menstruate" again, without taking hormones, get the cause of the bleeding checked.

Middle Age, however defined, has two real attributes— it is often the real "prime of life" in that one can then do and enjoy things not possible at other times of life for lack of experience, money and know-how; and it is, in our day, the repeat of adolescence, in that it involves grappling with the identity crisis preparatory to the second half of life. Women have this crisis dramatized by the menopause, as adolescence is dramatized by the menarche. Men have no menopause, but between forty and fifty they are forced to reassess their success in attaining goals. The "male menopause" is a gimmicky title for the second identity crisis in males. It has no basis in biology and merits decent burial as a phrase, for there is no male hormonal change as sharp as that which occurs in women.

We enter adolescence with realized fantasies, derived from good parts of childhood, which we wish to perpetuate or reachieve, and unrealized fantasies, which may or may not come to pass or to prove rewarding if they do. Middle age has both these components, plus the frustrations of the unrealized, and the unsatisfying when realized—its whole shape can be altered, however, when we shed the mythology of impending decline. The sixteen-year-old who feels "on the shelf," because he or she has never made it with a girl or boy, needs reminding that there is plenty of time. The middle-ager needs reminding that forty is halfway and the identity crisis is the start of the second trajectory, an idea which the poisonous folklore of age tends to conceal. Like adolescence it is an opportunity.

"Prudent" adolescence would be the preparation for adulthood—only adolescence runs to being experimental, not prudent. Middle age is the preparation for active seniority and can be prudent if we don't panic. Women in particular find venomous and near insoluble problems if they are confronted with sexual reassessment in a society which rules the older woman sexually noncompetitive. Some of these problems can at least be faced; others, like impending retirement-unemployment, can be actively dealt with by preparation. An altered mood toward aging and an awareness of what aging does and doesn't involve could greatly modify the present second-crisis experience by removing the panic pressure arising from the social expectation of decline. Most old people would have prepared differently for the second trajectory, economically, educationally and personally, if they had realized what age would actually be like.

The expectation of an age in which intellect, sexuality and activity remain very largely unimpaired for a long time takes the pressure off middle age. It does not and should not remove all the pressure, for the rethink is

> To know how to grow old is the master work of wisdom, and one of the most difficult chapters in the great art of living.
>
> Henri Frédéric Amiel

salutary, even if we opt for a pattern in which the second trajectory is the linear continuation of the first, as is the case with old country men and women who don't experience any sharp crisis like ours. In a protean society, middleagers, like teenagers, are an identifiable group, needing a rite de passage; the menopause is a biological rite of this kind, and can be liberating. Men are in need of a social equivalent, leading to a moral retooling. Without it there is a risk of getting sick or thrashing around. A truer view of age and what it holds is an important preventive against a bad second adolescence which mistakes itself for obsolescence.

Militancy. According to modern gerontology, some 75 percent of what we now call "old age," viewed as an accumulation of penalties and disabilities, is a product of institutions and of attitude, not of biology. The remaining 25 percent, which is a product of biology, may incapacitate us and will eventually kill us. But it is the unnecessary 75 percent on which we can most profitably concentrate in the first place.

In terms of this, programs for older citizens, however excellent their intention (and in most cases the intention is excellent, and better than their execution), are, like all "welfare" programs, aimed basically at pacification, or keeping the natives quiet, without having to change too many things. The more things one has to change, the harder it gets politically to push programs through, and the more expensive they get. Recognizing aging as sociogenic is a big change—it's an idea that has not occurred to most people, in or out of Congress or government agencies.

If those who are now old and those who will be old intend to turn this around, they need clear objectives, not only in terms of specifics, but also in terms of the basic change in society's thinking and practice which they want to effect. The basic changes are that no social or other penalties shall be incurred by the passing of time, and that the disabilities incurred through illness at any time of life should have a safety net put under them. In other words, we strike the word "older" from the phrase "well older citizens" and from the phrase "sick or disabled older citizens." We liquidate oldness as something of which society takes cognizance, except insofar as it involves entitlement (which is what happens

Maggie Kuhn was sixty-four in 1970 when she organized the Gray Panthers, a network of highly vocal older people around the United States who are dedicated to fighting agism. Ms. Kuhn, a firm believer in experimenting with new lifestyles, was living with two women in their late twenties when she was sixty-nine. "One reason our society has become such a mess," she said, "is that we're isolated from each other. The old are isolated by government policy."

throughout life in cases of promotion and insurance maturity). This means that we strike "age" off public documents except for statistical or record purposes, in the same way as the Constitution requires that we strike "race" or "religion" off public documents except for those purposes. Entitlements remain—you have to do X for a certain time in order to get Y—and this may make optional retirement an entitlement, as in the military, but nobody should be forcibly rendered unemployed. Whether this would entail a constitutional amendment against age-based discrimination or an extension of the Age Discrimination in Employment Act by striking the sixty-five-year limit is a matter for practical examination.

As to the real disabilities of age, they need the assistance proper to the real disabilities of *any* age. To a socially age-blind philosophy the support needs of the frail, arthritic or brain-damaged person of eighty are not generically, although they may be practically, different from those of the frail, arthritic or brain-damaged person of twenty-five except that actuarially they can be expected to be needed by the old in greater numbers, but for a shorter period of time.

Some older people may be scared that age blindness will expose them to the cold and to the loss of special treatment. (The welfare income of older people has actually risen more than that of younger people.) This is a mistaken view. Age is a period of earned entitlement, certainly, but then it is not a period to live needlessly on welfare. Pacification and stopgap programs may "help the old," but they don't help them to avoid black magic effects: being sent back to work during World War II did. If people are to be cured of thinking they have undergone a rite de passage and become different people, it can only be on a basis of taking "age," meaning number of years lived, out of the reckoning and keeping in "need," which is a measure of real ill health or disadvantage, and is independent of age. If you are in a wheelchair or have heart failure you may need social support, whether you are twenty, thirty, forty or ninety, and the support will be roughly similar.

The pretext uses of age, which function now as copouts for everyone, would also be lost—people would no longer be fired because they were x years old; they would not be reappointed on grounds of incompetence or of ill health, which would at least be honest. This particular wind would be tempered a little to the shorn lambs, both employing and employed, by a continuance of term contracts and pensions, but backed by a second-trajectory job program (see *Retirement*). The detailed implications of striking age from the record will have to be thought, and probably fought out just as the implications of striking race are being thought and fought out. But this is the objective—that no citizen shall be terminated, penalized or demeaned solely as a result of reaching a calendar date, and that there shall be support for citizens, regardless of age, who are unable through disability to support themselves.

Attitude-altering attempts do not belong to the province of government. They can be the province of education and the media, however, and both of these will need the ageless conception of people dramatized to them by argument and, where necessary, by protest (see *Media*). Realistic black characters on television and in movies have done more to solace the resentment of black people than to promote integration; the sight of black TV news reporters being in their places and doing their jobs as a normal part of the landscape has probably done a great deal more. The media can easily project

George Burns was born on New York's Lower East Side in 1885 and within seven years a career that was to illuminate the world of comedy had begun—in a youthful street-corner quartet. For forty years his name was inseparable from that of his wife and stage partner, the beloved Gracie Allen. After her death, in 1964, when he was expected to retire, he instead became even more involved in work. In 1975, when he was eighty, he co-starred in the film *The Sunshine Boys*—and won an Oscar.

agelessness. In Britain, for example, the BBC's gardening expert Fred Streeter ran a weekly program at the age of ninety-eight. It is cardinal to this kind of "consciousness raising" that people in later life are seen or heard publicly and efficiently doing their offices in health and with mental vigor and competence, not as jolly exceptions kept as pets by society, but as the norm for that period of life, and unexceptional as fit younger people are unexceptional.

There is a traditional belief, which has substance, that older people are conservative and that Americans, with atypical exceptions, reject radicalisms. They are probably wise to be so and to think in this way. The limited "radicalism" of rejecting age prejudice, like the radicalism which rejected race prejudice, is not a vehicle for any political ideology, only for the assertion of neighborliness. A nation of immensely neighborly people has somehow come to discount a part of itself as true neighbors. In the case of racism, the blame lay with history and with barriers which had stood for a long time. In the case of the old, there is no such barrier, and what barriers there are have been constructed during our lifetime. They are alien to the general political sense of America—in some unforeseeable way "the old" have somehow ceased to be included in the ideology of enterprise and reward, of independence and of citizenship involving participation. Getting them put back in their rightful place seems to be a conservative rather than a disruptive operation; it is the exclusion of some 15 to 20 percent of the community from active involvement in any activity, from producing wealth to pursuing happiness, which is the disruptive innovation. The forces of inherent neighborliness ought to be strong enough to set this right, but the attention of society is going to have to be drawn to what those people need and are not getting.

We may at some stage have to fight off the risk of performance pressure, which has operated on past occasions over many matters, and could lead to a state of affairs where older people faced the same demoralizing performance anxieties which now invade sexuality, some reaches of business and education, and even Women's Lib (as an insistence on particular life-styles both for women who would by inclination prefer a traditional option and for those who reject it). Realistic nonagism is not a denial of the fact that there are physical age

Marian Hart, flying a single-engined Beechcraft Bonanza, completed another solo transatlantic flight in 1975—at the age of eighty-four. Ms. Hart, who had flown more than five thousand hours, learned to fly in 1945.

changes or that these are unequal. It asserts that those who wish and who can, should be permitted to do and to continue doing, with branch options based on the cashing of entitlements for those who wish to take them, and full support for those who are unable to continue. The essential thrust of such a view is in the normality of continued engagement compatible with one's health and inclination, and this rubric applies at any age.

There are obviously also senior rights specifics which need asserting now, as the Gray Panthers are asserting them. These do not involve contradictory pleadings (that old people are no different, and that old people need protecting). The point is that people are being ripped off and mistreated, and, in this instance, those so dealt with happen in modern society to be old. A lot of legislation is on the books which would palliate existing abuses if it worked. It can be made to work by citizen pressure. Work, housing, transit schemes, abuses and rip-offs, such as those of nursing homes, crime protection and tax inequities, and the creation of a health service to replace the commercial sickness industry, are all goals or targets for this kind of pressure.

In taking militant action—that is, in making protest or in campaigning in a way which is audible, visible and inescapable by authority—seniors have immense practical advantages. The chief among these are leisure (they do not lose a day's work or classes if they meet or march), experience (often in conventional law, politics and the like) and respectability. While on occasion they need to be willing to shout, they have resources beyond shouting; consider the effect of a mass visit by fifty seniors on a bad nursing home or to a do-nothing official and you will see the potential for consciousness raising. Noisemaking is an important but minor political weapon in a democracy. Lobbying, petition drives, voting down candidates or bond issues, filing class actions, sitting on boards of neighborhood bodies, registration drives and the potential, if it can be realized, of a 15 to 20 percent senior block vote are all democratic expedients springing from the fact that the over-sixty-five group, if they can be galvanized, have now the inestimably valuable weapon of free time. While black activists needed a national drive to register their voters and legislation to prevent interference, most senior voters are registered already.

The sole reason that this massive political clout does not now land is that "old" voters tend to be isolated. Of the major senior organizations, one is into insurance salesmanship, while the other is into Democratic and union politics, and both, being nonprofit bodies, are

Bob Hope, born Leslie Townes Hope in London in 1903, was awarded the Congressional Gold Medal by the United States Government in 1963, a unique accolade for a comedian. Hope made his name in radio, underlined it in Hollywood (in more than fifty films) and confirmed it—if confirmation were needed—in television in which he celebrated twenty-five years in 1975. To tens of thousands of ex-servicemen, he is remembered as the man who would go anywhere, however remote, to entertain them.

precluded from rough-and-tumble political campaigning. That leaves the Consultation of Older and Younger Adults, alias the Gray Panthers. In their manifesto Maggie Kuhn, who organized the group, wrote: "We did not select our name, the name selected us. It describes who we are: (1) We are older persons in retirement. (2) We are aware of the revolutionary nature of our time. (3) Although we differ with the strategy and tactics of some militant groups in our society, we share with them many of the goals of human freedom, dignity and self-development. (4) We have a sense of humor. Our purpose is to celebrate the bonus years of retirement as a time for contributions to the new age of liberation and self-determination." Exemplary, certainly. The radicalism which sees all people as ageless is a novel one, even among professional radicals of other stripes, and will need some preaching.

Reformers are people who want to alter the attitudes of society. Radicals are angry people who want to alter the attitudes of society. American institutions are alterable, albeit slowly, through democracy and the extrademocratic power struggle. Attitudes require other means of reform, but when they change societies change with them. There is basically no honorable or rational interest which would be infringed, no principle of public policy which would be prejudiced, no economic danger which would be incurred and no person who would be hurt by the entrenched recognition in American society of the irrelevance to a person's rights of the length of time he or she has lived. It is rather the reverse, for in times of external emergency we adopt that position, only regressing to folklore in times of business as usual. It is inevitable that older citizens to come, who will be ourselves grown old, will alter this backsliding. Prudent forecasts will recognize this certainty, whether they are the forecasts of business, of government or of the political parties. Like racism, agism has had its day. It is not only idiotic but also anachronistic, and "the old" to come will not accept it. The reforms they demand will not disrupt but will strengthen the society on which they are imposed, however little that society likes them at the time.

There is an occupation ready for every retired, unemployed American. Wherever two or three people are gathered together to promote these changes, there should he or she be in the midst of them.

Mao Tse-tung emerged as the
leader of six hundred million
Chinese in 1949, at the age of
fifty-six, after years of constant
struggle, first against the
failing Manchu dynasty, then
the Japanese and finally against
his erstwhile ally, Chiang
Kai-shek, whose armies he
drove into exile in Taiwan.
More than a quarter of a
century later, and in his
eighties, he was still the "great
helmsman" of the world's
most populous nation,
ideological luminary for
radicals throughout the world
and the man two American
presidents traveled across the
world to visit.

Mobility is not fully appreciated until for any reason it is compromised. It is worth noting the magnitude of the effect the next time you have a sore toe.

Mobility can suffer with aging as a result of the increase in such ailments as arthritis, and also from general weakness, both of which do not so much stop one from getting about as taking the active pleasure out of it. In later life, too, quite minor handicaps can suddenly become monstrous if, for example, they compromise getting down stairs or onto buses.

Over vast tracts of the United States mobility means the use of a car. Take that away and your entire life strategy may collapse. It is vital when retiring not to bet too heavily on the mobility you then have, even though in fact you keep it. Loss of driving power and of agile walking power are contingencies which should be thought about in planning (also what happens during a prolonged power failure or an elevator strike).

Towns with usable public transit systems may give concessions to seniors, and provided they design vehicles so seniors can get on them without hazard, are a mainstay of independence for them. In Europe this arrangement is general. There is, for example, virtually no place in London you can't conveniently reach by bus. In America, of respondents in the Chicago area 67·7 percent over sixty-five used the CTA bus, and another 5·0 percent other buses, although 11 percent had cars and were licensed drivers. Not all cities have good public transit.

Most futuristic rapid-transit schemes aim to carry commuters without clogging the streets. In view of their importance to those unable to drive or to walk long distances, consideration of these schemes as services for seniors is vital. You can build a splendid monorail and put it up three flights of steps a nonmobile person can't scale, thereby putting the entire system out-of-bounds to a main service-consumer group. Good public transit reduces everything from sickness (because services are accessible) to malnutrition (because stores are accessible) for an entire swath of seniors. One-man-operated buses can exclude them if the driver either can't help people on, as he usually can't, or can't see clearly when they are on and secure. The authority may not recognize when there is nonuse for this reason or because of bad design of the access step, because after one tumble or failure to mount many older folk go home and count buses out thereafter. More original senior car-pool or commuter-computer schemes would be a possibility if someone were to fund them. This is now occurring in some cities. Meanwhile, pressure needs to build first for good public transit, and second for the transit provided to be of a type that semi-mobile people can readily and safely use. This would enormously increase the range of life strategies open to older citizens.

Florrie Ball, a motorcycle enthusiast from Lancashire, England, thought her cycling days were over when she was seventy-seven years old and her insurance company, discovering her age, refused to give her coverage. Ms. Ball, who had been a motorcyclist for twenty-six years and could still tackle a two-hundred-mile trip with ease, tried unsuccessfully for a year to get insured. Finally an insurance broker, hearing of her plight and taking into account her completely accident-free record, arranged for coverage.

Muscles and Strength. Muscle loss is a normal age change. It is greatest in inactive people, and a lot of folk who become "tired of life" are in fact tired, period. The best preventive of disabling loss of strength is continued steady exercise, although experiments have shown that fairly drastic hormone supplementation alone can reverse senile loss of muscle. Exercise is the better bet. At his eightieth birthday party, Charles Atlas, the strong man, was still tearing up telephone directories (showing, incidentally, how skill comes to stand in for strength in later years). A good set of medical gymnastic exercises *arranged by an expert* can pay off at any age, not only in preserving muscle, but also in effecting retroactive hormonal benefit and lowered blood pressure. The really determined person will keep in training if possible, or will at least remain deliberately active.

Nursing Homes. The Gray Panther movement organized "guerilla theater" in August 1975 in Atlantic City for the benefit of the convention of the American Medical Association. One skit showed a doctor auctioning off old people to nursing-home proprietors in the audience —the Kill 'Em Quick Home, the One Nurse Home, the Way to Heaven Home.

Nursing homes now occupy the place of fear for old people which was once occupied by the workhouse. Unlike some primitive tribes, we do not kill off our aged and infirm. We bury them in institutions. Commercial nursing homes can be operated for profit by anyone with the cash to start one. They house three-quarters of all old people in America who are in institutions, the rest being either in nonprofit or governmental old-age homes; many of these are run by religious or fraternal organizations and vary in quality. But even the quarter in these nursing homes may, in some cases, have to be moved to a commercial facility if they are really sick, because a nonprofit home often does not have medical facilities for them.

Money-making homes (the industry prefers the word "proprietary") are possibly the sharpest point of confrontation between the idea of a medical service and the reality of a sickness industry. Dr. Robert Butler defines a nursing home as "a facility that has few or no nurses and can hardly qualify as a home." There is a minority of excellent homes of this title in which care is genuine. There is a host of expensive but abominable homes in

There is nothing more remarkable in the life of Socrates than that he found time in his old age to learn to dance and play on instruments and thought it time well spent.

Montaigne

which food, sanitation, medical facilities and, above all, any treatment of the inhabitants as people are totally inadequate. Most seniors who read the occasional but typical scandals in the press know this, view "nursing homes" with terror and disgust and rightly see them as the anesthetic room of the crematory or the funeral home. This assessment seems well-founded.

Most American nursing homes for the old are staffed, according to Utah Senator Frank Edward Moss, with "people off the street, paid minimum wages, who have no training and are grossly overworked." Wages are a big drag on profits, and even one skilled nurse costs money. In the interest of convenience, all civil rights (to privacy, sexuality, keeping one's own money and even one's own clothes, making phone calls) tend to be surrendered at the door. Most homes are in practice segregated. Of residents, a high proportion are women, victims of their naturally longer survival, and most are poor, although they may only recently have become so through outliving their savings. A fair proportion, if they were rich, could live in a hotel. Some patients have chronic brain syndrome, either real or aggravated by despair and by lack of stimulation, or some other grave disability. About one-third could have continued in the community with minimal help, except that the help wasn't administratively available.

Nursing-home care is extremely expensive, both for the private citizen and for the public agencies which often pay for it. Oddly enough, the origins of the new gold rush lie in Social Security, which put money into the pockets of the old, enabling them to buy the residential care given prior to 1935 by poorhouses and the like. Nursing homes and the battery farming of the old rocketed into a four-billion-dollar industry and became a growth stock, with average profits on investment of about 15 percent until rising costs started to cut down first on food and services, and eventually also on margins.

The trouble about checking out a nursing home, if you are forced to deal with one, is that in most areas you are unlikely to find one which survives the check. Good ones in any case have waiting lists which only VIPs, relatives of the proprietors and stockholders are able to jump. Items to check include food, fire hazards, whether "patients" are up, dressed and active, or needlessly in bed or in nightclothes, the existence of privacy and private property and whether the staff knows the

He that has seen both sides of fifty has lived to little purpose if he has not other views of the world than he had when he was much younger.

William Cowper

patients' names. A good dodge, on behalf of a prospective entrant, is to approach the owners as a potential investor and see what sort of a spiel you get about the low costs, high profits and high turnover. Not all bad promoters are justiciable crooks, but in many cases you could be excused for being fooled.

Congress and several states have attempted to do something about this state of affairs, but as 74 percent of the twenty-four thousand homes in the country were found deficient in 1971, legislators have a problem; if they enforce proper standards and put the slave traders out of business, they will abolish, or price out, all residential care for large sections of the community. Pressure on the states from HEW and various measures of reform all run into this unspoken roadblock. The real solution, if the taxpayer knew it, is to get public money out of the commercial old-age industry and put it into community created and supervised centers with both resident and day-care facilities (possibly linked to the Veterans Administration, which now has a big gerontology program) and into home-care schemes, some of which themselves employ able seniors, linked to protective housing to enable the citizen to age in his own home. Staying in one's own home is the top gerontological objective after continuing participation in life. For any homes which still exist as closed institutions, the ombudsman proposed by the Nixon administration should be constantly around to prevent the virtual imprisonment incommunicado of inmates. This would be a minimum program. It would collect the extra 15 percent now going to waste. In the meantime, staying out of the hands of nursing homes and rescuing elderly people from their proprietors' clutches rate high in the task of avoiding the worst kind of end to life. You wouldn't voluntarily put a relative in Belsen or go there yourself.

Picketing by seniors' organizations, not only of bad nursing homes, but also of the houses and offices of politically active citizens who own or have stock in them, is a retirement occupation much to be commended. Steady your aim by finding out solid facts about the really bad cases, and tell the media first.

Officials and the Runaround. Officials, both public and commercial, are supposed to be there to act for you (after all, you pay them), but the older you get, the less some of them act that way. Most people *will* be helpful and conscientious, but you may meet the odd, insecure functionary who conceives it to be his public duty to economize at your expense or to make you work for your various rights and entitlements by giving you the run-around, or who tries to take unfair advantage of you. If a few older citizens are courteously but immovably persistent, these characters can be turned around. Read the story of the Importunate Widow in Luke 18: 1 for technique and strategy. Cultivate elephantlike gentleness with immovability until you get results.

In England there are voluntary, self-help groups called the Claimants' Union. A little old lady goes to some public office for her entitlement—and gets told to walk four miles to a post office for a form they don't have. She goes to the Claimants' Union. The next day she returns with an attorney. If no joy, she comes back the following day accompanied by a mob from Rent-a-Crowd. Quieter and more civic versions of this can be organized, but only if older citizens get together.

One doesn't normally need to go that far. Ordinary foul-ups (computer systems which cannot read mail and keep misbilling) respond rapidly to complaints made to a newspaper or a radio "action reporter." Most of the time public officials are there to help and will do so. Make full use of your local Area Agencies on Aging. (See *Resources.*) The limits upon what public agencies can do are far more often due to their structure and to funding than to lack of concern of the people on the spot.

Pets, because they are age-blind and don't answer back, often make better company in an agist society than most people. Pets are no substitute for people, but they can lighten loneliness. You may then get nearly as heavy a physiological reaction from the death of a pet as to bereavement, including quite serious illness from guilt. Unlike relatives, we often put down aged dogs and horses, and the repercussions of this on you can be far more severe than you expected. Don't have a pet you will get attached to, but may not be able to exercise, afford to feed, leave behind to make visits or take abroad. A beloved dog sometimes cuts an old person off from traveling and from doing other things he or she might do to remain fully engaged. Don't substitute a pet for living or use one as part of "old" role playing.

Franz Liszt, the nineteenth-century Hungarian composer and concert pianist, was approaching seventy when he began to write his most remarkable music—works which anticipated the style of such twentieth-century composers as Debussy and Bartók. The greatest piano virtuoso of his time, in 1886, when he was seventy-four, he toured Europe and gave a number of brilliant recitals until two weeks before his death.

Poverty. Statistics indicate that apart from the obviously prosperous, not all old people in America are poor. In the study done by the National Council on Aging, 15 percent over sixty-five gave "not having enough money to live on" as a major problem—which means about three million needy people. The real outcome of this study is that a high proportion of those who are poor in old age have always been poor or nearly poor, and around this single factor of income flock all the other vultures, from bad health and shorter life expectancy to bad housing, exploitation and fear of crime. More prosperous and semiprosperous older citizens seem genuinely less afflicted by low income than younger people (often they are more economical and experienced, and many lived through the twenties and thirties) and others are genuinely surprised by the benefits they get. A good self-image, health, physical activity and the ability to get things done are greatest in people with a decent income. In consequence, to him or her who hath shall be given, and from those who have not is often taken away even that which they have. There is not too much correlation in old age between income and education, compared with younger ages. Retirement tends to flatten income differentials, while educational differences remain.

The self-defense measures recommended by old people themselves in the same study are noteworthy—making sure you will have medical aid available, saving and learning about pension and other entitlements lead the list. Many regret that they didn't plan second careers before retiring, or obtain more education when it was available.

There has in fact been an overall rise in the purchasing power of older people. The 70 percent rise in six years, from 1969 to 1974, in Social Security payments at least offsets inflation, and the proportion of "aged poor" has undergone a striking fall, even though incomes in the over sixty-five age group run on the average at about half those between forty-five and fifty-four.

This, however, is what might be called the official and political view. It is true that older Americans are doing rather better than before, and some of them say so. On the other hand, if you reckon the difference between buying a becoming dress and some dress, between being able to visit children and not being able to, and between living in reasonable comfort and having to line up for food stamps, anything up to half of our seniors are short of funds, and most of these, in contrast to the Federal and official "poor," have got that way as a direct result of age.

Dr. Robert Butler in his book *Why Survive?* has outlined the tortuosities of official computation which allow an old couple to buy "1 percent of a new sofa per year." We need to be leery of the adequacy of social security programs on which we shall not be compelled to live until we are old. Like it or not, society still penalizes age as age—granted "the old" are more economical, they had better be, as their incomes are only a half to a quarter of what they were. Adequate money is the most important single thing which separates a good from a bad old age and a healthy from an unhealthy old age, and the gains there have been, which are real, have to be kept rolling, not only by constant pressure from the old, but also by the conscience of society, which paid millions of dollars toward the education of its children, the results of which now disappoint it. It has now to be ready either to pay millions of dollars to settle its debts to those who built its prosperity or to wait until it is made to do so by newfound senior militancy.

Moreover, what a government official thinks a statutory person can get by on isn't necessarily the same as an adequacy. The manifest poverty which does occur, in all places and in all ethnic groups, in spite of past thrift and past labor—simply through outliving diminished savings—is demeaning. It is also wearing. It comes at an age when one has lost some of the resilience to fight hassles, to deal with relief officials, to line up for entitlements or to fight a court case, and all of the ability, by the decree of society, to go out and earn money, even when one still could. There is plenty of fuel here for indignation and for trying to turn society around.

Enough money is the thing older people need most. Many do not have it; society will not let them work to get it, and some are unable for physical reasons of incapacity to earn it in any case. Either we give it to them, or we had better obligingly set up one of the clinics which Kurt Vonnegut describes in *Welcome to the Monkey House,* which operated as a kind of walk-in restaurant, gave you a free meal and slipped you a dose which killed you. Euthanasia by attribution and inanition is nastier and more inhuman than this would be. Yet that is what we have got, so long as we insist that after a certain age one may neither earn nor receive a real

❝From the nineteenth century onwards the numbers of the aged poor became very great, and the ruling class was unable to pass them over in silence. In order to justify its brutal indifference it was forced to undervalue them.❞

Simone de Beauvoir

adequacy, but must go on trying to get it, getting one's exercise from the welfare assault course, but with failing vigor and growing exasperation. A lot of good work has certainly been done for the old, but it is not enough to buy society a communal halo, and we are kidding ourselves (or politicians are kidding us) if we think that it is.

Much more than in some other countries, where old age is a poverty trapdoor, poverty among old Americans is not so much a special issue as part of the general issue of social justice and the common wealth, carried into old age, and at a general standard of living higher than anywhere else.

At an earlier age, you could, if you were lucky, fight poverty by working harder—a tactic most employers would approve of, provided there was work and you weren't declared redundant. The only way older people (and, in fact, if one looks at it realistically, any unprivileged people in a profit society) can fight poverty is by organization and by militancy. This is coming up fast. It's no coincidence that some Gray Panthers are old union organizers. The difference is that the old are asking for payment for work they have done, if not for work they are doing—a fair demand, and one which is going to have to be met, even if it lowers the living standards of younger citizens.

Prostate. With the passage of time the prostate gland commonly enlarges in males. What causes the enlargement is not clear; sexual excitement without orgasm has been alleged to aggravate it, and sexual activity to prevent it, but there are no reliable statistics. If the prostate enlarges much, it may block the outflow from the bladder, first producing frequency of urination and then difficulty in making water, a problem requiring surgery.

Prostatectomy is safe and can be done at any age if health is good. Done properly, as a conservative operation, it removes a nuisance and a danger. (The obstruction won't just "go away" and will finally become complete, with an ongoing risk of other kinds of mischief to the waterworks.) Prostatectomy, done properly, need not affect sexual potency, although it sometimes alters the sensation of ejaculating or even abolishes ejaculation. Radical operations cut the nerves controlling the penile hydraulics—and these can indeed produce impotency. You should discuss the consequences fully with the surgeon; find out exactly what he intends to do and why. A surgeon who values his own sexuality won't wantonly compromise yours, but you should lay it clearly on the line, in case he shares the common illusion that you are or should be sexually retired.

Almost all old prostates contain areas which look like cancer under the microscope. Probably they are not truly cancerous, for they seem to do no harm. Real cancer of the prostate requires surgery, but it is one of the easier cancers to treat, since the secondary deposits in other organs, which are the main problems with cancer, can be controlled in many cases by giving female hormone. This does turn off libido, and you may in this case have to choose: bone secondaries can be painful and disabling, and untreated cancer will kill you.

Pulling Rank is one of the pleasures of age to which you are entitled, so swallow what you have learned about modesty and nonassertion and use it. It could be considered part of "assertion training for seniors." Courteously and immovably show people that you value yourself and expect them to do the same. Be ruthless to rudeness or brush-offs (see *Dignity*). If you have disabilities point them out to airline clerks, bus drivers or salespeople, and specifically ask for help—if you were an old VIP they'd offer it; you are entitled to it as a privilege of being old. Maybe you can't be a Chinese grandparent and impose deference, but at least you can cash the stamps you've collected in many years of useful life. Most of the time you will not have to make waves, and will be agreeably surprised at the way neighborly people go along with the idea that you merit respect, but *usually you have to show you expect it*; often people fear that help will infringe your independence. You may not need help, but if you do, it's an entitlement, not an imposition—that is what fellow humans are there for. When you are not of an age to pull rank, you are there to be neighborly to seniors, so help those who are.

❛The spiritual eyesight improves as the physical eyesight declines.❜

Plato

Coco Chanel, the Parisian dress designer who retired in 1938, made a triumphant comeback in 1954, when she was seventy-one. For seventeen years, until her death in 1971, she ran her Paris salon and remained firmly established as the twentieth century's single most important arbiter of fashion.

Quackery. Quacks are the least of most older Americans' problems because, apart from a few dollar-size rip-offs like phony health foods and bogus diet bestsellers, they aim at the rich. One wouldn't bother with them if they only fleeced incautious millionaires, although millionaires, too, have a right to know what can and can't improve their aging. Occasionally, however, quacks sell to people of moderate means who can ill afford it. Accordingly, it's worth knowing the main sales pitches.

Any clinic, remedy, system or what-have-you which (1) claims to slow down or prevent age changes, (2) involves odd pseudoscientific concoctions such as embryo extracts, royal bee jelly and "vitalized" preparations, (3) has to operate outside the United States to avoid the Federal Drug Administration and the laws about mail fraud and (4) either charges luxury hotel rates or pulls the "pay what you feel you can afford" spiel, is fraudulent quackery designed to ring changes on the goldbrick trick. Quacks can be qualified or unqualified—some believe in what they are doing, others believe that there is one sucker born every minute—but their aim is not to rejuvenate you, it is to enrich themselves.

Not all the most modern techniques for reducing age disability are available in all parts of America, because there is as yet no comprehensive geriatric hospital service on the European model. However, the facilities do exist in some places—Long Island Jewish Hospital in New York or the Baycrest Hospital in Toronto, Canada, for example, and there are many others. This type of center attacks aging by first-class preventive and curative medicine followed by rehabilitation and a strong social follow-up, since it's pointless to cure illness and then send you home to an intolerable domestic setup. A good family practitioner trained in geriatrics does the same thing on a continuing basis, because with you he plans a continuing strategy to head off physical problems, to cure those which occur and to adjust to any which can't be cured. Such a geriatrician reads the current medical literature, knows what is new as it comes along and will usually be willing to try anything which might do good and is demonstrably not going to do harm. This is real geriatric medicine, and it has no gimmicks.

Quacks, too, quite often do good. If they have any sense they raid the armamentarium of proper geriatrics (providing pleasant surroundings, psyching-up, making you feel wanted, giving exercise, imposing rules to make you feel you are on a new trip) but they supplement these, which actually do any of the good which is done, with the equivalent of gold-coated pills, for which you pay through the nose. Most of these remedies are what are called placebos (they make you feel better because you have paid for them and expect something) and you would get as big a charge from ground-up subway tickets. A few have some "fringe science" justification, but no demonstrated value—if they had, they'd be in general use by conventional medicine.

Here are some of the lines in unorthodox pharmacy most often exploited by quacks. The sell can be quite soft, "You understand we don't talk here about rejuvenation, and we can't promise to help your problem, but in our experience we often can and so, etc., etc."

Royal jelly. Vitamin-rich material fed by worker bees to a bee grub to make it develop into a long-lived queen, not a short-lived worker. It, therefore, lengthens the life of bees. There is no evidence whatever that it lengthens the life of anything else—or removes wrinkles from the face, breasts or any other part of the body. Cost, as a cosmetic, whatever you are fool enough to pay.

Cellular therapy. A long-standing sales pitch, very popular in Germany, and based on injecting you with a minestrone made ostensibly from live sheep-embryo cells, and popularized by the late Dr. Niehans. The old idea seems to have been that the cells took root and grew, but the pitch grows a new "scientific" basis every time the last one is exposed as hogwash. The latest basis is that the miracle results from DNA, RNA or enzymes in the cells, which has the advantage that extracts are even more expensive than homogenized baby sheep. (A recent superpitch, a particularly lowball approach, is to start rumors that these mixtures cure Down's syndrome in children.) There is no serious clinical evidence of the value of cellular therapy other than testimonials and anecdotes and no scientific basis of any kind in terms of modern gerontology. Cost, if you went to the late Dr. Niehans' Swiss clinic, 2,800 dollars to 3,000 dollars for one week, including board and treatment. The FDA has trodden on this one in America, but there are several European and Mexican points of sale, most of them run by people to whom you wouldn't send a St. Bernard.

Recipe for Youth
❝On the seventh day of the seventh month pick seven ounces of lotus flowers; on the eighth day of the eighth month gather eight ounces of lotus root; on the ninth day of the ninth month collect nine ounces of lotus seeds. Dry in the shade and eat the mixture and you will never grow old.❞

Yin Shan Cheng Yao

Another arm of the operation is that to choose your mess you have to have a whole rack of expensive pretests ("Aberhalden tests") to see which sheep constituents you are supposed to lack. It's worth knowing some of the jargon just in case what looks like bona-fide geriatrics starts moving in this direction, at which point, if you have any sense, you leave, ignoring any bills which are sent to you.

KH3, "Gerovital." This is the dental anesthetic procaine, used as an antidepressant for older people. Not quackery (see *KH3*), but often pushed by quacks. The test here is what is charged and whether there are any fancy extras. Now under proper test—if found to be useful you will be able to get it from your doctor at about one dollar a shot.

Other funny-money biochemicals include such things as raw chick embryos. Some clinics don't use any of these suspicion-raising techniques. What they actually give you is a sensible regime of diet, exercise, getting away from it all, European spa treatment, physiotherapy and some resident hookers thrown in. One could get all this for one-tenth the cost nearer home, but it is a hassle to set it up and, like Naaman the Syrian (2 Kings 5 : 12), you are paying for the magic. The old-fashioned European spa had much to commend it. The mineral water and the baths were for the birds, but it put the older person in a structured situation, away from home and turmoil, with a change, company, controlled food and exercise and often some kind of magical ordeal, like drinking nasty water, to perform. These are quite effective forms of magic, and it would be worth making them cheaply available under medical supervision, as some European countries do.

Most quackeries at two thousand dollars a week are an insult and are irrelevant to people getting five thousand dollars a year. But even if all of us could afford them, or get them for free, "rejuvenation" of this sort is not for those with real physical aging problems. It is rather for people anxious about their body image, overfat from self-indulgence, unable to accept themselves as people of the age they are and sexually anxious, with such inner-generated consequences of that anxiety as impotence, which they blame wrongly on age, but which is really due to attitude. A rich man or woman who wanted to age well would, if sensible, go to a good geriatric hospital like those we've named. A satisfied rich man or woman might thereupon use money, influence or both to endow the start of a voluntary geriatric service for everyone, while lobbying for a Federal service. In Britain and France, which spend respectively 6 percent and 7 percent of their GNP on seniors, geriatric services like this exist, and in Britain are available (although not yet in all areas at a high standard) as a right. Given that, anyone who pays two thousand dollars to Dr. Rip-Off in the Cayman Islands is an accident looking for a place to happen—"thus do knaves make game of fools."

Records. People have always enjoyed the fantasy of going on living for almost always. When as a child I found out about dying I used to pray to live to 110, which seemed more likely to be granted than praying to be immortal. Anecdotes about the very old have always been popular. Thomas Parr, who died at a reputed age of 169 and was buried in Westminster Abbey, unfortunately had the life tenancy of a cottage, and was probably father, son and grandson, the village going along with the mystification.

There are several problems with old records, aside from the fact that we want to believe in huge ages. These include mistakes in dates, two people of the same name of different generations, the tendency of all humans to recount as experiences what they were told by others. "I heard about the ride of Paul Revere" gets to be "I actually saw the ride of Paul Revere." In particular, there is the old habit of renaming a second son for his father when the first has died. Edward Gibbon, the historian, had a second brother, also Edward—the writer was a sickly child and had not been expected to live.

Allowing for all this, and the huge treatise by William Thoms in the nineteenth century, pointing out the unreliability of a lot of old-age stories, the calculations proving it impossible to live to be more than 105 have not stood up to birth certification. Many people do exceed that age (although whether so many well-fed people brought up driving and living in cities will do so is anyone's guess).

The oldest person with a near watertight claim to the world title for Being Around is probably a shoemaker

6No wise man ever wished to be younger.9

Jonathan Swift

167

called Philip Joubert. He was born in Charlesbourg, Quebec, in 1701. In 1814, when he was about 113, he thought himself to be only 105. It is not known exactly when he died, but if, as is believed, he died on November 18, 1814, that made him about 113 years 100 days. John Turner of Tottenham, London, died on March 23, 1963, aged 111 years 281 days. He had had to stop work because of failing sight, but at his 111th birthday party appeared as a tall, thin, blind man who looked about 70. His own comment was, "I am not an unusual man—just one who has lived an unusually long time." Mrs. Ada Roe of Lowestoft, born in Islington, London, died on January 11, 1970 aged 111 years 339 days. She ran a dairy store, and worked in it until a few weeks before her death. These people had watertight birth certificates checkable against other documents.

There may be even older people around. Some of the oldest in the United States have no such records; innumerable surviving "Civil War veterans" have turned out to be old soldiers of a different kind. The most interesting title claimant is Charles Smith of Bartow, Florida. According to the American Medical Association and the Social Security Administration, he was, in 1972, the Union's oldest inhabitant, having been retired from a citrus farm in 1955, at the age of 113, as too old to be permitted to climb trees. Smith said he recalls being lured on board a slave ship in Liberia, where he was born, at the age of 12, and being sold in New Orleans to a white man called Smith. His exact age was undocumented, but the part of the story that can be investigated stands up. That would make him close to 130.

Every discussion of supercentenarians turns at some point to the inhabitants of three places—Hunza-land in the Himalayas, Abkhasia in Georgia, U.S.S.R., and Vilcabamba in the Ecuadoran Andes, where huge ages have been reported. Leaving out Hunza-land, where there are no good age records and part of the story may have rubbed off James Hilton's novel *Lost Horizon*, the actual ages reached in these communities are difficult to verify. (Ages from 140 to 168 have been claimed in Abkhasia, but it is known that in these regions ages were adjusted regularly to avoid the Czar's draft.) What is true is that in relatively prosperous Abkhasia and in impoverished Vilcabamba age makes no social difference to the role, participation, sexual activity, work or other activities of the aging person, and in these circumstances there are few decrepit oldsters and many incredibly vigorous centenarians.

Allowing that diet and possibly genetics help, it is tempting from these and from similar communities with less extreme high-age claims to infer that decrepit age is largely a sociogenic effect. True, in remote mountain areas like these, where in the past there have been no doctors, a lot of people who began to fail died of illness or accident. Those who didn't die, however, never saw a time-based reason to stop doing exactly what they had always done for as long as they could do it, and one finds a similar history in sporadic people like ex-slave Charlie Smith. Whether such folk stayed alive because they never were obliged and indoctrinated to quit, or never quit because of a totally unusual endowment which we can't all attain, is something well worth study; it is the main use, indeed, of "records." Other than this, nothing can be gotten from comparing the prescriptions of the long-lived for survival, but it is important in demonstrating the way in which we are "shaped" to "grow old" at an age when hairy peasants in remote areas are in midlife vigor.

6Youth, large, lusty, loving—
youth full of grace, force,
fascination,
Do you know that Old Age
may come after you with
equal grace, force,
fascination?9

Walt Whitman

Charlie Smith ran a small store in Bartow, Florida, until he was 133 years old. In 1955, when he was 113, he was made to retire from his work on a citrus farm because he was considered too old to be climbing trees. In 1972 he was officially recognized as the oldest person in the United States. The father of an octogenarian son, Mr. Smith lived alone at the back of his store until 1975, when, on medical advice, he moved into a retirement home.

Relatives. One consequence of contraception, of changing family habits and of a falling child death rate has been a shortage of kin, compared with the large traditional human family. The "extended family" on the Jewish, Chinese or Italian model has been overpraised—as well as mutual support, it generated pressures we now are unwilling to accept. Apart from the fact that one of numerous nonlib daughters could be drafted, often to her lifelong hurt, to "look after" older relatives, the great advantage of the extended family in later life was less its size than the cohabitation and intermixture of generations. With urban housing this was bound to decline anyway. The surrogates for generations sharing a house are the car and the telephone, but these don't provide constant interaction for the old with grandchildren, who become only occasional visitors. The older dynamics of the three-generation family have effectively disappeared.

Relatives, especially children, are people on whom you are perfectly entitled to rely for support of many kinds, but the folklore of independence has much that is valid in it, and children when adult aren't necessarily the people you most want to talk to. The real need of older people is for friends rather than the relatives of earlier peasant-type societies. Dr. Jacob Bronowski, the author of *The Ascent of Man*, remarked that Americans tend to be friendly, but friendless. In fact, all ages seem to be in a social transition from relationship-based to friendship-based social bonding. The ideal outcome of this, envisaged by Tolstoy, Thoreau, the early Christians and the hippies, is the "all people are brothers and sisters" formulation. This, however, remains hot air unless some quite powerful charismatic interaction takes place. At present we lack the use of straightforward concern, which gets neutralized by "independence" as an ideal in America and by "privacy" as an ideal in Britain, and do not universally draw bonding from religion—the nearest approach is through parareligious behaviors like humanistic psychology and the encounter group. At the same time, the void left by kin is widely sensed, and probably accounts for the appeal of "growth" movements among middle adults, and even the quite extensive reappearance of the Eskimo expedient of wife exchange, the aim of which is in fact to create surrogate kin, by one of the strongest types of primate bonding.

We cannot now predict how the children of this transition period will age. They will certainly be more peer-

6 When you are old, you feel like a grandfather to all small children. 9

Victor Hugo

172

dependent and less kin-dependent, they may still go to encounter groups rather than to churches; ideally, if society is by then age-blind, the active extrusion of each generation by the next will have gone. In the meantime, grandparenthood is and will remain as basic a human learning experience as is parenthood, both for child and for grandparent. In all cultures good grandparenting tends to limit parent-child overexposure, which is particularly onerous in our isolated small-family households. Being an active grandparent is one continuing responsibility of seniors which they should hang on to, difficult as the institution of serial polygamy may make this. Children in general like the company of grandparents. They also like to hear about the past, and telling them about the past has a function, so don't confuse this with doting reminiscence. This is how tradition is passed on. Every wise young parent will involve grandparents to the full. Even if you fear that your own parents will be overindulgent or oversevere to your children, remember that exposure to a different set of child-rearing ways is highly beneficial to children as a learning experience in the diversity of people. Since few children who don't live with them get overexposed to grandparents, comprehension between grand-generations is often high.

Try to avoid leaving your own solution of the kinship/friendship transition until retirement. Work masks isolation, and in our work-dependent society the illusion collapses at retirement. You risk being left as a kinless and friendless couple or individual. "Friends" moreover require a more definitely shared peak experience than playing golf, drinking cocktails or belonging to the Shriners, to constitute or bond them.

Jomo Kenyatta said, "I do not know when I was born, what date, what month or what year." He was, however, probably in his seventies when, in 1964, he became the first President of the Republic of Kenya and the cornerstone on which his country's national history will be built.

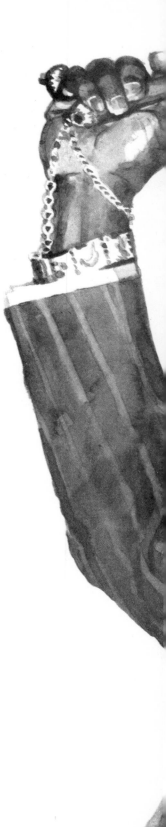

Religion. "Old" people, since they are supposed to be "near death," are also supposed to be "religious" to an extent that young people are not. In fact, surveys show that older people for whom religion was important in youth find it still important in age. In other words, they are still themselves. Others, of course, discover—or lose—religious faith as they make other kinds of discovery in the journey of experience. By "religion" we mean a delimitation of the experience of Self in dialogue with what is Not-Self, which appears to be its deepest psychological and philosophical meaning. If so, the very fact of experience continuing, but being at some time soon about to cease, does puncture our tolerance of triviality and "bad faith." Some of the strongest trends to self-discovery have occurred in therapy groups devoted to people who know they will soon die.

Not that the years after sixty-five, any more than those after twenty-five, are normally spent in the contemplation of eventual death. Age, however, has real occasions for self-knowledge if people take them. The "future" does inevitably shorten—which means that the present ceases to be trivial and fit to waste on marketable trivialities. By sixty-five you begin to realize that you have spent too much time in Disneyland. Experience begins to emphasize quality, something our culture demeans. Age is the only vantage from which you can see the shape of your own life cycle, instead of saying that your personal history is bunk, and rushing on regardless. One has to deal with satisfaction and regret; where there is remorse or guilt it is less often neurotic and more often based on past errors of judgment. Also, most people want to leave a legacy, whether it be genetic, practical or simply that things won't be as if they themselves never existed.

While not "religious" in the sense of compelling adherence to a major religious tradition, these experiences of normal maturity are congruent parts of the self-confrontation which worthwhile religious experience involves. At any age, one may elect the mystical or quietist form of self-exploration as the most apt for one's experienced needs, or the devotional, or that offered by an existing and tried tradition. Often the fully realized older person who has undergone personal growth doesn't retire to tell beads, but rather, like a bodhisattva, stays "in" the world raising radical hell for the rights of others, including others who are less fortunate.

6And fire is seen in the eye of the young
But it is light we see in the old man's eyes.9

Victor Hugo

Nobody is getting the best from "religion" who joins a religious body purely for company, but religious bodies, both Catholic and Protestant among Christians, and the whole community of Jews, offer a kind of fellowship which fights against the societal classification of "the old" as unpersons, and for this they deserve maximum credit even from the unbelieving.

Death is a source of interest in genuine religion only to the extent that it detrivializes life. "Immortality" was never, except in vulgar error, a religious concern—Christianity in its orthodox form teaches resurrection, and Judaism doesn't teach it at all. Later life is, accordingly, not spent in "preparing for Heaven," but in understanding the Self, a far more genuinely religious enterprise.

Resources. One problem about American programs for seniors is not that they are lacking but that they tend to be multiple—federal, state and local. Accordingly, it takes research in any given area to find out what is being done and what isn't. The place to start this is at the town library, if you are a book person, or, if you are not, at one of the Area Agencies on Aging set up by a State Office on Aging under Title III of the 1973 Amendments to the Older Americans Act. The Older Americans Act is well worth reading, because it shows exactly what Congress has authorized. Its Title VII, for example, authorizes nutrition programs, and many of these are in existence.

Entitlements are like insurance payments. You worked and paid for them. You don't refuse to collect insurance, or your pension, under the mistaken impression that these represent charity or welfare. The robust independence behind that attitude is something to respect, but the attitude is mistaken. Accordingly, find out what is available. These are services like the police and the fire department. You pay for them, and you're entitled to call on them.

Some of the following special services (the list is not exhaustive) may exist in your area. If you could use one of them, find out if they do exist. If they don't, find out why not. At a recent meeting of a Board of Supervisors, when a "senior" issue came up, the gallery was full of seniors. When their spokesman had made their point, he called on the public to stand up and turn around, and each had chalked on his or her back the number of years they had lived in the county. They got their decision.

Area Administration on Aging (who should know all the answers.)
Home repair, yard work
Day-care centers for infirm elders
Transportation and escort
Legal advice
Nursing-home ombudsman
Communal meals
Meals-on-Wheels
In-home and homemaker service
Low-cost senior housing
Senior employment agency
Free clinic
Primary care physician trained in geriatrics
Old-young bridge-building projects; foster grandparents
Communal purchasing and mutual-aid organizations
Senior social center
Chapter of AARP, Gray Panthers, etc.
Special services for sickness and disability,
such as recordings for the blind,
counseling for the terminally ill. You probably
don't need these now, but some people do,
you may, and they should be in place.
Education; entry to local college and university programs
Outreach; bookmobiles, nutritionmobiles,
paramedic and medical inhouse services
Influenza immunization
Public transportation concessions
Senior rates at entertainments (theaters, concerts, sports)
Telephone counseling, like the "Dial SENIORS" scheme in Illinois

There are two kinds of service here—those for the fit, and those for the unfit who often aren't able to lobby when they need the service. The assignment of fit seniors, who are the majority, is to get these fallback mechanisms operational through civic pressure.

One useful legacy of World War II in Britain is the Citizens' Advice Bureau—usually with a main-street shop front—where one can take any request for information, and which acts as a general crisis management center as well. Although it doesn't and shouldn't deal only with seniors, a bureau of this kind could be an early and extremely useful project for any senior-power organization in a district where there is nothing equivalent, running on retired attorneys, bank managers, social workers, councilmen and informed citizens generally as a permanent panel with the duty to stay updated so that they can function. It could usefully add the action-line function discharged in Britain by another less official body, the Claimants' Union, which acts as a hit squad for the victims of rip-offs, bureaucratic and otherwise, by providing pickets.

There are resources about, and where there aren't, they can be got by informed, persistent, orderly pressure. The golden rule is to find out ahead of time—so that you know what there is, and can lobby for what there isn't and ought to be.

Retirement. We can only alter the manipulative cost-accountancy concept of retirement, which kicks people out of society when they can't be milked further, by changing society. On the other hand, from the standpoint of self-defense, retirement has to be met, unless you are wholly self-employed, a housewife, an intellectual of a certain kind, or a peasant—these people never retire or don't notice that they have.

Ideally, retirement isn't the occasion for leisure, unless the work you did was incredibly arduous and not even then, for "leisure," as packaged by golden-age promotions, is Dead Sea fruit; you can read and play shuffleboard just so long. However much he grumbled about the hassle of daily work, the man who without knowing it had all his friends and most of his significance at work usually enjoys about a week of staying at home, although breaking habits and lowering tempo are disorienting even then. If his wife isn't working outside the home he gets under her feet. If he tries to do all the jobs he has put off until retirement he commonly finds that his strength or his heart, if his work was sedentary, protest. A man who had been doing heavy work will quite often go on doing it at home.

Women in the conventional order, who if they worked were in reality expected to hold down two full-time jobs, are in fact protected from some of this because there is no retirement from "homemaking." But the more the sex roles come to resemble each other, the more the problems of men and women are becoming similar.

Sad things happen to retirement fantasies—the

6 Youth is the time of getting, middle age of improving and old age of spending; a negligent youth is usually attended by an ignorant middle age and both by an empty old age.9

Anne Bradstreet

couple who withdraw to a mountain cottage they'd seen in summer, and find that in winter they get snowed in and there are no food or mail deliveries; or there is simply the fact that when the fantasy home, or trip, comes it's unreal and not a part of living, however tiresome living was. Nest eggs which looked huge when laid may prove good for only a couple of bites after twenty years of inflation. Only two kinds of folk are really happy conventionally retired—those who were always lazy, and those who have waited a lifetime to get around to a consuming, nonfantasy interest for which they have studied, prepared and planned, lacking only the time to do it the way they wanted.

The first self-defensive move is some introspective reprogramming about achievement. In American folklore, all movement is upward. If you stop moving, you are by definition dead. The man who goes from clerk to salesman, to chief salesman, to manager, then to a seat on the board, is actually on a trapdoor—if he gets to be company president, there is nowhere further to go, unless he is aiming to be elected Pope. Therefore he stops moving, and therefore he is a failure. This is a major piece of white-collar nonsense, and its victims are apt to retire beaten men, or get promoted beyond their abilities and suffer from depression if that happens. When they don't work, blue-collar people tend to suffer from a loss of company and from a deep loss of self-esteem. No number of gold watches or managerial compliments can be substitutes for some special dignity as craftsmen emeriti, and retirement feels uncommonly like ordinary unemployment.

You can turn these attitudes around in yourself and use them constructively if you realize that retirement *is* unemployment. This is the most self-preserving attitude for anyone who is in good health and even for many who are not. It's no use, after all, if achievement has been your guiding light, to try telling yourself that you've achieved and can now sit on your backside, unless you are really comfortable with that posture. If you are not, then the objective in retirement is to go on achieving, but without the pressures of having to do quite as much as in your first trajectory, and with more opportunity, often, to make the achievement yours rather than the corporation's. If your sense of dignity, of manhood or of womanhood depends upon the fact of working, that is a worthy conviction, so act on it.

Fred Streeter, Britain's most
famous gardener, made his
first radio broadcast, a short
talk on runner beans, when he
was fifty-eight years old. He
quickly established a unique
reputation as the BBC's
gardening expert. A gardener
since he was twelve years old,
he had a tremendous knowledge
of plants and flowers and never
needed reference books nor
used a script for his weekly
broadcasts. His familiar voice
was heard by millions of
listeners only a few hours
before he died at the age of
ninety-eight.

Helena Rubinstein created and built up over seven decades a beauty empire that stretched across six continents. In her memoirs, *My Life for Beauty*, written when she was in her nineties, she said, "But work has indeed been my beauty treatment. I believe in hard work. It keeps the wrinkles out of the mind and the spirit. It helps to keep a woman young. It certainly keeps a woman alive."

Early on, you have to analyze for yourself the meaning of money. You need to get rid of irrational feelings about getting money. What you have earned you have earned, and any entitlements society offers you by reason of age or because it has put you out of a job *you have paid for*. So far from being charitable gifts which demean you if you take them, these benefits are your earned rights and you should raise hell to get all of them to finance your next career.

This attitude is important, because the strategy of retiring into work, the second trajectory, depends upon two types of planning. One of these is financial, so that you can live, bearing in mind that work by the retired is penalized and paid negative wages by society. The other is prospective, so that you have both skills and an outlet for them set up and ready to move into, not more than two weeks after your first trajectory ends. Two weeks is about the ideal length of time to retire.

In examining achievement, don't be overinfluenced by what it has meant for you in the past. If your achievement has been organizational a lot of it will have been laid on you by other people. There are busy tradesmen who retire to devote all their time to painting or to chess and these outlets genuinely meet their needs. But be a little cautious of reliance on hobbies. While they can represent a new trajectory, society has a way of selling them to keep the unpeople quiet, and they don't contribute to society. Such preoccupations are good for you if they truly express a part of your identity which hasn't had time for expression. For most people actual working activity in society is a great deal better.

The way things are programmed, and particularly in a recession, when there are not enough jobs for those who haven't been retired, there is plenty that retirees can do provided they will do it for free, or only for expenses. Clearly you have to avoid being used to cut down other people or to lend credence to the idea that older citizens are there to do the scut work, at cut rates. In some cases, if you do get paid, you lose benefits, which in a rational scheme would be yours by right of your previous labor.

Accordingly, the defensive strategy is, first, to have set up what you will do *before* the year of your retirement (and preferably you will be doing some of it, so that you are run in, as it were, when the second trajectory begins). Second, if you have problems, try to avoid going it alone. A group operation by a number of retiring or retired people has a broader base than an individual effort. Make full use of any local senior citizens' employment organization if you want; go it alone if you must. But at least do as ambitious younger men and women do—plan a trajectory and get on a launching pad. The consciousness that this is not a replay of, or a fall from, what has been done before, but is rather a second, distinct life is probably the most important preparation to resist being dumped from society to become a frustrated passenger.

One occupation open to everyone who shares the spirit of the Founding Fathers is full-time political and neighborhood activity on behalf of the rights of all persons, and of older persons in particular. It may not be a paying occupation, but it can extend you to the full, and there's nothing like fighting to provide healthy exercise.

Remember that people show a frightening tendency to deny what aging in our society is like, particularly financially. In a recent study of one thousand reasonably prosperous, nonretired people between the ages of thirty-five and sixty-five, 90 percent said their present income wasn't adequate, but 86 percent reckoned they would have an adequate retirement income, although

❝If you are smart and manage to stay healthy, you'll also stay smart, although it may take you longer to demonstrate that fact at sixty-five than it did at twenty-five, and the print in which the questions are written may need to be larger.❞

Ward Edwards

on retiring their earnings would be cut by half. In fact, even apart from inflation and the growing risks of ill health not fully covered by Medicare, you actually use less money when you work full-time than when you are not working. If you are not working you spend more, and the jolt is bigger than more retiring people anticipate.

The alternative to cultivating the second trajectory (and to shaping society so that educationally, financially and in all other ways it becomes universally accepted and available) is to have twenty-nine million idle and un-employed Americans by the end of the century—the number who will then be over sixty-five—(more if we shorten working life any further). Ancient Rome ended with slaves doing the work and most of its citizens living on handouts, but it's not a good mixture for a civilized democracy.

As we have said, the proper time to initiate self-defense and rethinking is long before you reach retire-ment age. It really belongs, in our society, to the period of so-called "middle age," around forty-five, which is now quite commonly marked by an identity crisis very like that of adolescence. Some people react to this climacteric by depression or illness, some by thrashing about or by breakaway action (new mate, new job). Not all of this turmoil is unconstructive, any more than is the turmoil of adolescence.

At present, with retirement set around sixty, the second identity crisis precedes the end of work by fifteen years. If retirement becomes earlier, however, there may come a time when the two coincide, and we shall then approach psychologist Thomas Lifton's protean life-style, with two separate trajectories each heralded by a period of identity-seeking and self-examination. We are in the transition toward this new pattern, which would be further reinforced if gerontology adds a slowing of the physical changes of age. In spite of the exploitive motivation which makes society push "retirement" into middle life, we may gain from this process if it concretizes the middle-life reassessment so that what it becomes is a renaissance.

The individual retiree is not strongly placed to find a new trajectory solo, but minimal group support can strengthen his or her hand—if there is no such support locally, your first occupation can be to get it organized. The Senior Citizens' Employment Bureau in White Plains, New York, interviewed four thousand retired

> ❛Young men are fitter to invent than to judge; fitter for execution than for counsel; and fitter for new projects than for settled business.❜
>
> Francis Bacon

Sir Barnes Wallis was eighty-three in 1971 when he retired from day-to-day involvement as Chief of Aeronautical Research and Development for the British Aircraft Corporation. But there were still committees to be served on, lectures to be given and new designs to be created. Behind him was a lifetime of visionary work in the field of aviation and air warfare, from successful airships in World War I and after, to the variable geometry (swing-wing) aircraft of the sixties, rejected in Britain, but successfully developed in the United States.

people in five years and placed 70 percent of them in gainful occupations, on an annual budget of sixteen thousand dollars, of which half was raised by donations and half by the local United Fund. Neighborhood groups could do the same on smaller budgets or by offering group-based services. Another technique is for groups to provide internal services—you don't need to live in a commune to rationalize your living through bulk buying, shared housing, mutual help and shared investment, and these things, which must be administered, generate employment. This, because it is of a noncompetitive, self-help variety, can be a new and enlightening experience for people who haven't tried it. Volunteer work is another outlet—provided that only those volunteer who see that as part of their trajectory and wish to donate skills to others; there is no room in the new image of aging for the notion that the old somehow "owe" unremunerated do-good skills to society,

Marc Chagall, the Russian-born artist, was seventy-four when he was commissioned to design the twelve stained-glass windows for the Synagogue of the Hadassah Hospital near Jerusalem. At the age of seventy-nine he produced two magnificent murals for the Metropolitan Opera at Lincoln Center in New York. In 1972, on his eighty-fifth birthday, the first French museum entirely devoted to the works of a living artist was opened at Nice—The National Museum of the Biblical Message of Marc Chagall.

but there is plenty of room for those who find personal growth in having time to help people, including their own peers.

The strategies then are: recognize that there will be two trajectories not one; prepare financially and organizationally for the second trajectory as you would prepare for unemployment; use every existing organization to achieve this; and create organization around you where there is none.

Professor Paul Weiss, who retired in 1970 from Yale University to teach at the Catholic University, was appointed to the Albert Schweitzer Chair at Fordham University and was then denied the job on the grounds of age; Fordham has mandatory retirement at seventy. Weiss sued for a million dollars and a declaration that the rule was discriminatory, pointing out that Schweitzer, for whom the Chair was named, did much of his best work when he was well over seventy and continued working until his death at ninety. In dismissing his suit, Judge Harold R. Tyler held that ability declines with age, and that age is not discriminatory because it affects all of us.

The Age Discrimination in Employment Act of 1967 extends only to sixty-five. One might possibly hope for a judicial reinterpretation of discrimination against age. Many Supreme Court Justices are and have been well over sixty-five. But even with specific legislation, it will take money to fight cases. Under the 1967 Act, Standard Oil paid a two-dollar age-discrimination settlement in 1974, and the pursuit of such cases could be a function of a national association for the protection of older people. At present 41 percent of those still working over sixty-five are self-employed, although there are major firms who hire seniors as a matter of policy and find them immensely successful. Although other countries—notably Sweden and Japan—recognize the economic value of the old more fully than does the United States, Americans are fortunate in the existence of a constitutional cast of mind so that legislation against agism, like that against racism, and even the writing-in of the right to work as a rider to the pursuit of happiness, are not unthinkable developments—after all, 20 percent of the electorate who will soon be old are more than have been affected by civil rights legislation to date.

There have, moreover, been some tentative public programs. The Retired Senior Volunteer Program had its funds held up in 1970 and 1971 by the Nixon administration, but it has considerable promise and is being revitalized. The Peace Corps, which of all bodies could use really experienced people, has only just over 1 percent of its complement over sixty. VISTA has done rather better (there are problems for older people in tropical or arduous conditions which don't arise at home) and SCORE, which provides retired volunteer counselors for small businesses, has probably done best of all. SOS (for senior volunteers) and Mainstream (for the chronically unemployed) have also provided work opportunities for the unwillingly idle retired. These, incidentally, are all programs which neighborhood action could have initiated but didn't—they stand to the credit of Federal agencies in doing something. It is argued by some that the Federal Government should be the employer of last resort in this and all cases. The constitutional adoption of the right to be employed, which may gain strength from a recession, would presumably oblige the government to be so, but for the meantime and aside from the agencies named, local group action is itself an employment, and that need not wait.

Rip-offs. Older Americans are favorite victims of fraud. (Probably the hoods share the popular view that they are credulous, and some are frail or easily confused by fast talk. Also, although they are not rich, they have some sixty billion dollars between them.)

Swindles are of all kinds. Simple ones include the bogus serviceman who steals when left alone, the bogus builder who says your chimney is about to fall and offers to fix it, and the individual who purports to be an inspector sent to exchange a wrong social security check, and tells you, "Sign here, please." Of medical frauds, the biggest lines are cancer cures, arthritis remedies, vitamin-tonic sales and medicines. For every dollar spent on research on arthritis, according to Dr. Robert Butler, about twenty-five dollars are spent, chiefly by older people, on fraudulent remedies. You can also get sold magazines, lifetime subscriptions to health clubs and all kinds of other expensive garbage by fast-talking characters who reckon you won't know your legal rights (and who become violent with old people if they are not paid cash).

Dame Edith Evans made her
first appearance in the London
theatre in *Troilus and Cressida*
in 1912 when she was twenty-
four. She made her first film,
The Queen of Spades, in 1948
when she was sixty. And when
she was eighty-seven she
appeared in *The Slipper and the
Rose*, a musical version of
Cinderella in which, in the role
of the Dowager Queen, she
acted and sang.

The only valid rule is never to sign anything and never to part with money at or from the door, except to salesmen you know. In many cases if something were worth buying, people wouldn't be employed to canvas. The place to buy goods and services is at a store or from a tradesman, after using the Yellow Pages and calling around to check prices.

Another operation tries to batten on your cash shortage by offering various bogus business opportunities or "home employments." Check anything of this sort with a consumer organization or the Better Business Bureau. Richer oldsters sometimes get visits or calls from bogus bank examiners. The idea here is to get a tap on your bank account.

One area to watch is the retirement-home business. Some retirement homes are genuine and give first-class value—a life lease of a condominium or an apartment with a down payment, monthly rental, some services such as meals, maid service and even nursing and social facilities—although most of these are expensive. Some are run by or for churches and are genuine. Others are straight but reputable commercial deals. Others are frauds. You will in any event have to put down some forty-five thousand dollars plus, say, five hundred dollars per month. The snags are: (1) no guarantee against an escalator clause "to cover inflation," which may lead to bigger monthly payments than you can meet and enable the owners to repossess; (2) no absolute security—if you go briefly into the hospital the agreement may let the owners resell the apartment without a refund of any kind; (3) bad services—some otherwise good-looking schemes purport to offer "medical services," but these consist of a resident nurse and a sickroom, occasional doctor's visits and the rest chargeable to Medicare in the usual way.

If you have the capital even to consider a move involving such a scheme, you have the money to get it checked line by line by a good attorney—otherwise you are simply hanging yourself. Reputable schemes will welcome this kind of check. It is not the same as verbal assurances from a salesperson, however charming. You need contracted services, a fixed rate of rental, total ownership of any property for your lifetime, including the right to sublet with the owner's approval, a reversion of part or all of the capital equity to you if you leave within a fixed period, or to your heirs if you die, and a contract which has been gone through with a fine comb by a sharp and cynical law office. Reputable schemes will give this (but don't trust their attorney—have your own). Any scheme offering free gifts, a chance "especially for you," free trips to Florida as their guests, etc., etc., is probably a swindle.

The answer to rip-offs is education. Smart older people already know to call the Better Business Bureau or, in extremes cases, the FBI. It's the weak who get ripped off. This is one area where older citizens' organizations are a protection—but some of these can themselves be rip-offs, too. Suspicion is a proper response to this kind of attack, so don't be scared of it. In Yorkshire they say "Tha wun't get King by trustin' folks."

Another favorite pitch is the high-pressure sale of hearing aids by an unqualified salesman who comes to the door with a whole box of tricks and gives a free "auditory evaluation." Some states are legislating to stop this. The hearing aid usually works, but it may not be suited to you—or you may not even need one, your ears may only need syringing—and the prices are way above those in a regular supplier's. Check any offers of this kind both with your doctor and with other suppliers whose names you'll find in the Yellow Pages. If you demur at a five-hundred-dollar pitch and the salesman discovers he has a returned hearing aid which is excellent and which he will let you have for only two hundred and fifty dollars, and is like the one he just bought for his own mother, place your thumb on your nose, slowly extend your fingers and show him out. Since 29 percent of people over sixty-five have some hearing loss (far more than have bad sight), this is a profitable racket. Treatment of deafness is a normal entitlement under Medicaid, so take it from there.

Sex. Aging induces some changes in human sexual performance. These are chiefly in the male, for whom orgasm becomes less frequent. It occurs in every second act of intercourse, or in one act in three, rather than every time. More direct physical stimulation is also needed to produce an erection. However, compared with, say, running ability, these changes are functionally minimal and actually tend in the direction of "more miles per gallon" and greater, if less acute, satisfaction for both partners. In the absence of two disabilities— actual disease and the belief that "the old" are or should be asexual—sexual requirement and sexual capacity are lifelong. Even if and when actual intercourse is impaired by infirmity, other sexual needs persist, including closeness, sensuality and being valued as a man or as a woman.

This view is, of course, totally contrary to folklore, to the view of society and to the projection of nursing-home administrators, some of whom disapprove of sexuality among their junior staff. It is even contrary to the belief of some older people, who have been sold a bill of goods. Luckily not everyone has so little sales resistance, and many older people have simply gone on having sex without talking about it, unabashed by the accepted and destructive social image of the "dirty old man" and the unsexual, undesired older woman. This takes considerable stamina, bearing in mind that those who are now eighty were reared on the sex education of the Victorians. As in so many other contexts, until recently the handicap has been self-propagating. Older people weren't asked in surveys about their sexual activity because everyone knew that they had none, and they were assumed to have none because nobody asked. Questions of this kind weren't asked by doctors either, because they might cause embarrassment, and they continued to cause embarrassment, although much less to the patient than to the doctor, because they weren't routinely asked. For some people, the fantasy of the asexual senior which they had when they were younger became a blueprint for their own aging, a classical case of bewitchment by expectation.

The figures on sexual activity for people over sixty-five are instructive. They show that older people are and always have been sexually active, but that they are getting less embarrassed about it as the culture gets less uptight about sexuality generally. As far back as 1926 the biostatistician Raymond Pearl found that 4 percent of all males between the ages of seventy and seventy-nine were having intercourse every third day, and another 9 percent were having it at least weekly. Kinsey's figures, published in 1948, pointed to a decline in coital frequency with age, but these figures were cross-sectional and did not give a lifetime picture for individuals. In 1959 Dr. A. L. Finkle and his team questioned 101 men between the ages of fifty-six and eighty-six who had no illness likely to interfere with potency. They found that 65 percent under age sixty-nine and 34 percent over age seventy were still active, with two out of five over age eighty averaging at least ten copulations a year. And this despite the fact that some of the sample had never had intercourse, others had had it only rarely and others, although potent, had no available partner. In the over-seventy group the main reason for inactivity was lack of desire, not inability to function—of all men over sixty-five only three cited "no erection."

More recently, Dr. G. Newman and Dr. C. R. Nichols questioned both men and women between sixty and ninety-three years of age and found 54 percent sexually active overall. There was no significant decline from past activity under age seventy-five; over seventy-five, 25 percent were still fully active, and the falloff was accounted for almost wholly by illness of the subject or the spouse. "Those who rated sexual urges as strongest in youth rated them as moderate in old age; most who described sexual feelings as weak to moderate in youth described themselves as without sexual feelings in old age." In other words, although attitude and possibly physiology play a large part, for some people "age" is a good excuse for dropping a worrisome function.

In 1968 at Duke University, Pfeiffer, Verwoerdt and Wang studied 254 people of both sexes. The median age for stopping intercourse was sixty-eight in men, with a range of forty-nine to ninety, and sixty in women, with a high of eighty-one, the difference being due to the age differential between spouses and the shorter lives of males. The figures for regular and frequent intercourse were 47 percent between sixty and seventy-one and 15 percent at age seventy-eight and over. This study followed the same people for five years, during which

6 Old ladies take as much pleasure in love as do the young ones. 9

Abbé Brantôme

time 16 percent reported a falloff of activity and 14 percent an increase.

What we are seeing in cross-sectional studies is a mixture of high- and low-drive people all bundled together; people for whom sex is a major resource and people uninterested or embarrassed about it and quite willing to lay it aside, people with unanxious and satisfying sex lives and people with long-standing dysfunctions. For those who have been happily active in youth, age abolishes neither the need nor the capacity nor the satisfaction, unless illness compromises their ability to enjoy sex, or deprives them of a partner—in which case they may well not wish to seek a socially disapproved outlet. Almost certainly the new old will score higher because they have grown up living sexually, and view sex positively, and have not aged in the folklore expectation of impotence and continence through incapacity, but in the determination to go on as long as possible in the style they have known.

The first step in preserving your sexuality, which for many people is deeply important in preserving their personhood, is to realize that if cultivated sexuality can be, and normally is, lifelong in both sexes. Women already know that the menopause, far from marking the end of sexual response, often marks a substantial upsurge of sexual enjoyment for its own sake, linked with the fact that one can now stop bothering with contraception. In women, hormone replacement therapy has cosmetic and physiological advantages and keeps the vagina in good condition, but frequent sexual activity has been claimed to be nearly as effective. Impotence in men has nothing to do with age; it is most often caused by performance anxiety, which can become disabling if you believe that age will affect your capacity. Impotence is more rarely caused by diabetes, and not infrequently by medication given to older people for blood pressure or other conditions, by injudicious surgery and by alcohol, which is a sedative. Remember, too, that your susceptibility to the "downer" action of alcohol may increase with age.

You need to be careful about both medication and surgery. If you suddenly lose either libido or potency when taking pills, check back with your doctor and if need be get them changed. If you are coy about sexual side effects the doctor won't spot them by ESP. Prostatic surgery (see *Prostate*) should not impair potency if done conservatively. Pelvic surgery in women doesn't usually interfere with sexuality at all, and, if it is for repair of sagging vaginal walls, can vastly improve sensation for both parties. In the face of surgery, discuss this aspect openly with the surgeon. There are still young men who do radical prostatectomies on seniors on the ground that "after fifty he won't need it" or advise that the vaginas of elderly women should simply be sewn up. Even these people, if confronted beforehand and put on notice, won't risk a malpractice suit, while a good and Hippocratic surgeon will cooperate with you fully in planning not only his surgical strategy but also your rehabilitation afterward.

Sex is a highly undangerous activity. Stopping it unwillingly is far more dangerous to health than a little exertion; in some people stopping leads to severe depression. Accordingly, abstinence from sex because of conditions such as a coronary or a major illness should be limited only to the time when you have actually to abstain from walking around the room. An old person who has an operation is got out of bed as soon as he or she recovers from the anesthetic, because bed rest in itself causes loss of function. This is equally true of male sexual function—one real age change is that if you drop your regular sexual activity for any length of time, you may have difficulty and need treatment to restart.

This disuse effect is often seen in widowers, when the wife dies after a long illness and the man wishes to remarry; here the disuse, the strange partner and probably some guilt at the relief natural when a lingering illness ends, can result in difficulty in getting an erection. In this case get help—the impotency is reversible by treatment. You need to defend your sexuality against both disuse and the assaults of injudicious treatment and advice—for this purpose you need a doctor with whom it can be discussed and who considers your wishes normal. Usually a doctor who fully values his own sexuality will value yours.

Age and society both lay burdens on women. For a start there are more widows than widowers, by reason of the "feminine advantage" in life span and the proneness of men to coronaries. (This may even up, if women continue to smoke cigarettes at an increasing rate.) There

❛I did not know that I could scorn women at twenty and be charmed by them at seventy.❜

Rodin

195

is also the fact—and it is a fact—that while a man of any age can attract a partner, and usually a younger partner, the older woman is subject to a sexual boycott. There is no easy remedy for this. Masturbation is an important sexual resource for both sexes at all ages, but it is not a substitute for being valued.

Probably the best defense is to enter age as a couple and hope that both of you die in the same accident. Experienced lovers, who take minimal care of their personal appearances, never cease to elaborate their sexuality and make up in proficiency and familiarity anything they may lose in looks. Sexual attractiveness has little to do with age and the appearance of a partner is a poor index of sexual skills. Both men and women need to avoid obesity, which is not only unattractive by our social norms but tends to interfere physiologically with erection. Cosmetic surgery can be of help when there are real problems, such as immense pendulous breasts which get sore, but its use is to restore function to the age you actually are, not to deny age. Most continued attractiveness is the outward and visible sign of inward and spiritual self-esteem. It's proper to use any means to stay active and to avoid sloppiness at any age, but don't be exploited by people who minister to your insecurities or sell you on your fears for sex follows upon how you are, not how you look; an experienced man would wish to have sex with a woman of any age close to his own who experiences herself as a fully sexual person.

There is a fitness in sexuality at all ages and for both sexes, but there is also absolutely no reason for society's jibes at marriage between parties of unequal age, which are usually directed more at the combination of younger man and older woman than the converse, and are often expressed in comment implying financial exploitation. If this kind of match arises in good faith and you know it is in good faith, treat society's and your relatives' remarks with the contempt they deserve. (Naturally, you will look out for gold diggers, and this applies whether you are a man or a woman.) Children can be highly critical or obstructive of parental remarriage late in life, sometimes in good faith and sometimes for fear of another long-lived heir. Tell them you did your part bearing or begetting them and press on. They don't own you and they have no right to lecture you. Unequal-age

No Spring, nor Summer beauty hath such grace, As I have seen in one Autumnal face.

John Donne

situations become unfit only when the older party loses his or her head. People of other ages are allowed or are expected to lose their heads when in love, but we are hard on the elderly who do so. Robert Burton in *The Anatomy of Melancholy* put it pithily:

> *Antient Men will dote in this kind sometimes as well as the rest; the heat of love will thaw their frozen affections, dissolve the ice of age, and so enable them, that though they be four score Years of age above the girdle, to be scarce thirty beneath. Otherwise it is most odious when an Old Acherontick Dizard, that hath one foot in his grave, shall flicker after a lusty wench. . . .*

True for both sexes, but among the new old, whose valuation of sex will be different, there will be fewer acherontick dizards of either sex.

The old who fare worst sexually are, as in other respects, those who through infirmity or for some other reason fall under the control of other people. Nursing homes appear to be run by people with sexual problems —otherwise it would be difficult to explain the attempt to run them as mixed-sex nunneries; a few even refuse to permit married people to share a room. More liberal advocates have talked about providing petting rooms for inmates. But what "inmates" here or anywhere else want is what is accorded to people at other periods in their lives—namely privacy and the right to establish relationships if they wish. What they don't require is a demeaning attempt to treat adults as children. They know their own minds and don't need their morals policed by busybodies who in turn regard normal sexual appetite in an older person as evidence of dementia.

It has been shown that residential homes which follow the sexual mores of the outside world, instead of those of a boarding school, have happier and less deteriorated customers, and a vastly lower consumption of tranquilizers, than the conventional "home." The sexual attitudes of such places are a good test of their general recognition that those they house are people and equal citizens, not cases for manipulation. It is possible that some of the segregative homes of the past did in fact reflect the mores of the older generation to which they catered. This is almost certain to change as the mores of society have changed.

Mae West was born in 1893,
the daughter of a prizefighter
turned livery-stable owner and
a corset model of Bavarian
descent. Always her own
woman, she created the image
to which she remained faithful
through more than sixty years
of stage and film work—a sex
symbol, vamp and flouter of
public morals (or so she was
accused). A superb comedienne,
she always wrote her own
material and chose her leading
men. Censorship on Broadway
and in Hollywood, it is said,
was invented to suppress her.
In her eighties, she remained
unsuppressed.

Sight. Far fewer people go blind during the aging process than become deaf, and most of this sight loss could be prevented. One absolutely normal age change is that the eye loses its ability to "zoom" as it does in youth, so that you need glasses—usually to see near objects. This is usually evident around forty-five and bottoms out by fifty-five.

There are three serious sight conditions which get commoner with age. One is glaucoma, in which pressure inside the eye rises because of obstruction of normal fluid drainage. Although painful later, glaucoma starts insidiously, often with seeing colored halos around lights. But it should never get that far, since a simple pressure test can spot it before harm is done, and it can be controlled by medical or surgical means. Checks for glaucoma are a part of every full medical examination, certainly after age forty. It is a common cause of blindness if neglected.

Another, rarer, disorder is senile macular degeneration, which is due to hardening and obstruction of the little artery which supplies the center of the visual field. The peripheral fields always escape; therefore, although the victim can see, as it were, sideways, the ability to read will usually be lost. This, too, can be stopped in many cases if changes in the disk are seen through the ophthalmoscope.

The third condition, cataract, is the major cause of blindness in late life. It is a progressive clouding of the lens, commoner in, but not confined to, diabetics. The first signs are trouble in seeing detail, seeing better in twilight than in daylight or in bright light, and seeing several moons when you look at the moon with one eye. Another symptom is being easily dazzled, rather as headlights interfere with your vision if the windshield is fogged.

Doctors used to leave cataracts to "ripen." Now it is agreed that it is important to spot them early, as early surgery gives the best results. But many patients are leery of an eye operation when they are seeing quite well and they take some persuading. The operation can be done as soon as you are blind enough to realize you have to have it. It consists of taking out the cataract, under general or local anesthesia. This leaves you with an eye effectively lacking a lens, and the surgeon will either put in a plastic lens, or, after the eye has healed, give you glasses. Of all cases so operated, 75 to 80 percent will be able to read with the operated eye. Probably if more cases were caught early the success rate would be higher, as some of the complications involve such things as retinal changes, which get commoner in the old.

Few older people go blind, but 60 percent of blind people are over seventy. Most of this blindness could be prevented.

Smoking. Cigarette smoking is one of the major life shorteners—not only because of cancer and of heart attacks, but because it damages lung elasticity and promotes bronchitis and emphysema, which lead to a wheezy, breathless and brief old age. It is well worth giving up cigarettes at any age. If you get bronchitis you will have to, but it is better not to wait for that. Whether older people lose the taste for smoking, or whether it is simply that those now old never smoked cigarettes heavily, we don't know. If your oral needs are strong, switch to a pipe, whichever your sex.

Supermarkets pose problems for older people living alone because they can't get single portions of many things, and they can't afford to buy larger packs and store them. Recently in Britain, where refrigerators are less universal than in America, pensioners who had to buy in supermarkets often went without some foods because they were ashamed to ask for one egg or one chop, not having money or storage space for more. This is a good example of what can be done by senior organization; many store managers when approached arranged to have split packs of such foods as margarine, eggs and meat for seniors at the meat counter or on a special stand where they could serve themselves. This is exactly what the neighborhood shop once did. But unless the need is made known, even concerned firms and managers can't be expected to meet it.

For the nonmobile, getting goods delivered is a problem. In our town only the most expensive grocery store delivers, and its prices run 25 percent over the supermarkets. Most nonmobile oldsters rely on neighbor cooperation, but a shopping service run by a group is one possible self-help activity for organized seniors; it could be combined with bulk buying and considerable cost reduction. The operative word here is "organized." You have to get together, with the help of your local seniors' agency if possible, to set anything like this afoot.

Claude Monet, the father of
French Impressionist painting,
embarked in 1914, when he was
seventy-three, on his most
important—and most ambitious
—project, a series of nineteen
huge paintings of water lilies.
These canvases, bathed in
shimmering, almost formless
colour, were the starting-point
of much modern abstract art.
Despite failing eyesight, which
required a cataract operation
when he was eighty-two,
Monet continued painting the
water lilies, and much else,
until shortly before his death
at eighty-six.

Telephone. This is the most important single technological resource of later life. If you can reach a telephone you aren't alone. Practice using it in the dark. And cultivate the habit of calling neglectful relatives collect—for their education, not for your benefit.

Free or reduced-rate telephone services are a more urgent subvention of seniority than are free passes on public transit systems and should be furthered.

Time. A lot of unhelpful attempts have been directed to defining different rates of time at different ages, as perceived by humans. Time has been said to creep in childhood, run in youth and fly in age. This could just as well be put the other way around.

What is true is that time, for a mortal organism, is the most valuable commodity. Experience and a period spent in using and wasting it at our own and other folk's instance make us capable of valuing it, so by later life we are capable of resenting triviality as never before. The age-categorization myth cheats us of about a quarter of the living time which properly belongs to us, by kicking us out of the "social space" which, if allowed by society, we could continue to occupy until our luck runs out.

A race of philosophers might manage to live nontrivially all its adult life, nontriviality not being the exclusion of playfulness but simply of the spurious, the meretricious and the not-worth-buying. A quiz-show cultural ideology resents the nontrivial, and even manages to trivialize something as august as long life, which most cultures respect, by retiring older folk and classifying them "no deposit, no return," as expendables generally devalue craftsmanship. Older people potentially represent a source of social quality control, and quality isn't one of our priorities.

The appreciation of time is therefore not a value we assimilate, but it is highly important to survival into "retirement" and the second half of our life trajectory; giving up and dying off are enactments of the finding that time is for us no longer worth having. The nonphilosophical people who show the sharpest awareness of its value now are members of psychotherapy groups for the terminally ill, who find out the hard way what time is for. Aging, especially good aging, is about the right perception of the human use of time, in the life cycle and from day to day. Here endeth the lesson.

❛Age, like distance, lends a double charm.❜

Oliver Wendell Holmes

Thomas Alva Edison, who attended school for only three months, patented a total of 1,033 inventions—the first at twenty-one, the last at eighty-one years of age. Much of the technology of the twentieth century derives from his pioneering work, from the electric light bulb and the generation of electricity to the microphone and the phonograph. Edison was seventy during World War I when he directed research in torpedo and submarine devices, and seventy-three when he agitated successfully for the creation by Congress of the Naval Research Laboratory, the first institution of its kind.

P. G. (Pelham Grenville) Wodehouse had an enormous literary energy that never waned. A London bank clerk turned humor columnist, he published his first story in 1902, when he was twenty-one. When he died, at the age of ninety-three, he had written more than a hundred books and was working on yet another.

Eamon de Valera was born in
New York in 1882, the son of a
Spanish father and an Irish
mother. He became Prime
Minister of the Irish Free State
in 1932, when he was fifty. He
served as President of what had
become the Republic of Ireland
from 1959 until 1973, two
years before his death at the
age of ninety-three.

Vitamins. Anyone living on a full and balanced American diet should not need added vitamins, and many of the preparations which are promoted as ways of safeguarding your health are expensive. On the other hand, there is evidence from studies of nutrition in older people that diets are not always as balanced as they look or as patients report. You will come to no harm by adding the approved standard daily dose of a full multivitamin preparation—ask the pharmacist for the cheapest brand, and check the correct dose with him and with the instructions on the bottle. Don't buy "megavitamins." Although some vitamins, such as C, are probably harmless in excess because they are excreted, others aren't.

The following instructive story appeared in *Modern Geriatrics*, January 1974. A daughter brought her seventy-nine-year-old mother to the hospital because she was "senile" (meaning demented and not talking to anyone) and wouldn't eat. She had the full investigative routine from keen young geriatricians, and many ingenious diagnostic tests were tried. There were no abnormal findings, except a raised blood calcium which led to a battery of parathyroid tests. While she was in the hospital the patient returned to normal, started eating, talking and reading, and finally went home. It was at the last interview with the doctors that the daughter casually mentioned "medicine." Some time before, it seemed, the mother had had pneumonia. Her own doctor was away and his stand-in prescribed ampicillin, and, as she seemed under par, chocolate vitamin pills, four a day. Partly because he was a foreigner, and partly because he didn't visit again, wires got crossed. He had said that the tablets were a tonic and good for her, not a medicine, so why not take more? The daughter bought them at two dollars and fifty cents for five hundred, and the mother was taking fifty pills, or 150,000 units of Vitamin D, a day. She liked the agreeable chocolate flavor. When the pills poisoned her, as they would, her mental blunting was taken as "normal for her age." Be warned.

Any unusual, expensive or very much advertised vitamin supplement can safely be assumed to be a rip-off. When in doubt ask your doctor what is the cheapest pharmacopoeial preparation of what he recommends.

War is the one major curse of our society from which, in prenuclear days, oldsters were exempt. The point of including it here is that wars are just about the only circumstance which makes our society take out its finger and drop its prejudices. It would not integrate blacks or treat them as people—until it needed soldiers. It would not recognize that women can be drivers, pilots and doctors until it needed person power. In the same way it backtracked on all the assumptions of agism when military considerations arose. For four years in Europe the "old" went back to the jobs for which they were supposedly past, and did them well. The "useless" and the "retired" manned first-aid posts, put out incendiary bombs and generally reentered society.

If we can treat "old" people as people in the interests of warfare, the possibility exists—although we show little sign of realizing it—that we could do so for the sake of doing it. After each war, women didn't wholly return to the kitchen or blacks to the ghetto. The trouble about age is that while these groups don't turn over with time, so far as identity is concerned, the "old" do. The postwar old are, therefore, a new group, who can't consolidate wartime gains. This merits our careful thought—how to get where society would happily put you if it ran out of soldiers.

The people, incidentally, who set about making wars have a way of being over military age themselves. Not always, but often. They're the same people who, although chronologically old, reckon they're exempt from the disabilities and hassle imposed on age-mates, and couldn't care less about them.

❧ When grace is joined with wrinkles, it is adorable. There is an unspeakable dawn in happy old age. ❧

Victor Hugo

Wrinkles are due to atrophy and elastic-tissue changes in the skin. They are accelerated by sunlight—the best way to get wrinkled all over is to be a fanatical California nudist. No medication or cream removes wrinkles, although you can paint over them with varnish or have them flattened out by plastic surgery. (The general effect of this, if wrinkling was very extensive, is that you have to bend your knees in order to smile.) Simple lanette wax moisture creams soften the skin. Buy them in jars from a low-price store. Twenty-five- and fifty-dollar jars of potted beauty are exactly the same product, with a smell added. Estrogen supplements may possibly hold off skin changes in women, but get a proper regime from a doctor. "Hormone" creams are of doubtful value.

Youth. One of the destructive features of agism is that it sets age groups against each other. The nastiest opposition to "the young" comes in fact not from "the old" but from jealous and resentful middle adults, who see (or fantasy) the "young" enjoying freedoms they missed or avoiding responsibilities they failed to avoid. Some of this hostility rubs off on "the old" via antikids or antistudent propaganda which identifies youth with irresponsibility, irreverence and violence.

Remember, it wasn't "the young" who staged Vietnam or Dachau. One thing modern American "young" do seem to possess, when they have the chance, is concern. If they do not yet show direct concern for the "old," that is largely because of noncommunication. The needed bridging is made harder by the fact that people don't become different people with age, so that if you, when old, introspect your youth, it will be the youth of, say, fifty years ago. It takes imagination to figure how you would feel if you were "young" now. It pays to find out if possible, although obviously you can't easily jump in. Meantime, while refusing put-downs on "the old," don't play the enemy's game by putting down "the young" or give up if communication is difficult and the noise-to-signal ratio is high. Youngness is, or can be, lifelong, and hopefully these young won't so often grow into adult rednecks and cold warriors as did their parents. You and they need to get together.

> For age is opportunity no less
> Than youth itself, though in another dress,
> And as the evening twilight fades away
> The sky is filled with stars, invisible by day.
>
> **Henry Wadsworth Longfellow**

Harold and Bertha Soderquist joined the Peace Corps in 1974, when he was eighty and she was seventy-six. The oldest volunteers, they were assigned to teach in a secondary school in Western Samoa. Although the Peace Corps does not expect volunteers over the age of fifty to do well in language training, the Soderquists refused to be let off the hook. "We went home and crammed," said Bertha Soderquist. "You pass with a one and we both got one plus."

The Prudent Diet

A fat-controlled, low cholesterol meal plan to reduce the risk of heart attack

The way to a man's (or a woman's) heart is still through his (or her) stomach, but the old saying has taken on another meaning; the food you eat can endanger your heart, or it can protect it.

The typical American diet is rich in eggs, which are high in cholesterol, and in meats, butter, cream and whole milk, which are high in animal, or saturated, fats. These foods tend to raise the level of cholesterol in the blood, and a high blood cholesterol level contributes to the development of atherosclerosis, a form of hardening of the arteries. Atherosclerosis is the condition that underlies most heart attacks.

For many people who show no evidence of having developed heart disease, the risk of heart attack may be increasing if their regular diet has been high in saturated fat and cholesterol. To reduce this risk, scientists recommend a meal plan that is low in saturated fat and cholesterol and still provides all the essential nutrients.

The diet which follows shows the moderate changes in eating habits that will usually be involved. It was prepared by the American Heart Association and has been reviewed by committees and doctors with special knowledge of the subject.

© 1972 American Heart Association

Follow the recommendations for number and size of servings

1

MEAT, POULTRY, FISH DRIED BEANS and PEAS NUTS EGGS

1 serving:
3–4 ounces of cooked meat or fish (not including bone or fat)
or
3–4 ounces of a vegetable listed here
Use 2 or more servings (a total of 6–8 ounces) daily.

Recommended

Chicken, turkey, veal or fish in most of your meat meals for the week.

Shellfish—clams, crab, lobster, oysters, scallops and shrimp—are low in fat but high in cholesterol. Use a 4-ounce serving as a substitute for meat no more than twice a week.

Beef, lamb, pork and ham less frequently.

Choose lean, ground meat and lean cuts of meat. Trim all visible fat before cooking. Bake, broil, roast or stew so that you can discard the fat which cooks out of the meat.

Nuts and dried beans and peas:
Kidney beans, lima beans, baked beans, lentils, split peas and chick peas (garbanzos) are high in vegetable protein and may be used in place of meat occasionally.

Egg whites as desired.

Avoid or Use Sparingly

Duck and goose.

Heavily marbled and fatty meats, spare ribs, mutton, frankfurters, sausages, fatty hamburgers, bacon and luncheon meats.

Organ meats—liver, kidney, heart and sweetbreads—are very high in cholesterol. Since liver is very rich in vitamins and iron, it should not be eliminated from the diet completely. Use a 4-ounce serving in a meat meal no more than once a week.

Egg yolks: limit to 3 per week, including eggs used in cooking.

Cakes, batters, sauces and other foods containing egg yolks.

2

BREAD and CEREALS
(Whole grain, enriched or restored)

1 serving of bread:
1 slice
1 serving of cereal:
½ cup cooked
1 cup, cold, with skimmed milk
Use at least 4 servings daily

Recommended

Breads made with a minimum of saturated fat:
White enriched (including raisin bread), whole wheat, English muffins, French bread, Italian bread, oatmeal bread, pumpernickel and rye bread.

Biscuits, muffins and griddle cakes made at home, using an allowed liquid oil as shortening.

Cereal (hot and cold), rice, melba toast, matzo, pretzels. Pasta: macaroni, noodles (except egg noodles) and spaghetti.

Avoid or Use Sparingly

Butter rolls, commercial biscuits, muffins, donuts, sweet rolls, cakes, crackers, egg bread, cheese bread and commercial mixes containing dried eggs and whole milk.

Every day select foods from each of the basic food groups in lists 1–5

3 VEGETABLES and FRUIT

(Fresh, frozen or canned)

1 serving: ½ cup
Use at least 4 servings daily.

Recommended

One serving should be a source of Vitamin C:

Broccoli, cabbage (raw), tomatoes. Berries, cantaloupe, grapefruit (or juice), mango, melon, orange (or juice), papaya, strawberries, tangerines.

One serving should be a source of Vitamin A—dark green leafy or yellow vegetables, or yellow fruits:

Broccoli, carrots, chard, chicory, escarole, greens (beet, collard, dandelion, mustard, turnip), kale, peas, rutabagas, spinach, string beans, sweet potatoes and yams, watercress, winter squash, yellow corn. Apricots, cantaloupe, mango, papaya.

Other vegetables and fruits are also very nutritious; they should be eaten in salads, main dishes, snacks and desserts, in addition to the recommended daily allowances of high Vitamin A and C vegetables and fruits.

Avoid or Use Sparingly

If you must limit your calories, use vegetables such as potatoes, corn or lima beans sparingly. To add variety to your diet, one serving (½ cup) of any of these may be substituted for one serving of bread or cereals.

4 MILK PRODUCTS

1 serving:
8 ounces (1 cup)
Buy only skimmed milk that has been fortified with Vitamins A and D.

Daily servings:
Children up to 12—3 or more cups
Teenagers—4 or more cups
Adults—2 or more cups

Recommended

Milk products that are low in dairy fats:

Fortified skimmed (non-fat) milk and fortified skimmed milk powder and low-fat milk. The label on the container should show that the milk is fortified with Vitamins A and D. The word "fortified" alone is not enough.

Buttermilk made from skimmed milk, yogurt made from skimmed milk, canned, evaporated, skimmed milk and cocoa made with low-fat milk.

Cheeses made from skimmed or partially skimmed milk, such as cottage cheese, creamed or uncreamed (uncreamed, preferably), farmer's, baker's, or hoop cheese, mozarella and sapsago cheeses.

Avoid or Use Sparingly

Whole milk and whole milk products:

Chocolate milk, canned whole milk, ice cream, all creams including sour, half and half, whipped, and whole milk yogurt.

Non-dairy cream substitutes (usually contain coconut oil, which is very high in saturated fat).

Cheeses made from cream or whole milk.

Butter

5

FATS and OILS
(Polyunsaturated)

An individual allowance should include about 2–4 tablespoons daily (depending on how many calories you can afford) in the form of margarine, salad dressing and shortening.

Recommended

Margarines, liquid oil shortenings, salad dressings and mayonnaise containing any of these polyunsaturated vegetable oils:

Corn oil, cottonseed oil, safflower oil, sesame seed oil, soya-bean oil and sunflower seed oil.

Margarines and other products high in polyunsaturates can usually be identified by their label which lists a recommended liquid vegetable oil as the first ingredient, and one or more partially hydrogenated vegetable oils as additional ingredients.

Diet margarines are low in calories because they are low in fat. Therefore it takes twice as much diet margarine to supply the polyunsaturates contained in a recommended margarine.

Avoid or Use Sparingly

Solid fats and shortenings:

Butter, lard, salt pork fat, meat fat, completely hydrogenated margarines and vegetable shortenings and products containing coconut oil.

Peanut oil and olive oil may be used occasionally for flavor, but they are low in polyunsaturates and do not take the place of the recommended oils.

6

DESSERTS
BEVERAGES
SNACKS
CONDIMENTS

The foods on this list are acceptable because they are low in saturated fat and cholesterol. If you have eaten your daily allowance from the first five lists, however, these foods will be in excess of your nutritional needs, and many of them also may exceed your calorie limits for maintaining a desirable weight. If you must limit your calories, limit your portions of the foods on this list as well.

Moderation should be observed especially in the use of alcoholic drinks, ice milk, sherbet, sweets and bottled drinks.

Acceptable

Low in calories or no calories:

Fresh fruit and fruit canned without sugar, tea, coffee (no cream), cocoa powder, water ices, gelatin, fruit whip, puddings made with non-fat milk, low calorie drinks, vinegar, mustard, ketchup, herbs and spices.

High in calories:

Frozen or canned fruit with sugar added, jelly, jam, marmalade, honey, pure sugar candy such as gum drops, hard candy, mint patties (not chocolate), imitation ice cream made with safflower oil, cakes, pies, cookies and puddings made with polyunsaturated fat in place of solid shortening, angel food cake, nuts, especially walnuts, peanut butter, bottled drinks, fruit drinks, ice milk, sherbet, wine, beer and whiskey.

Avoid or Use Sparingly

Coconut and coconut oil, commercial cakes, pies, cookies and mixes, frozen cream pies, commercially fried foods such as potato chips and other deep-fried snacks, whole milk puddings, chocolate pudding (high in cocoa butter and therefore high in saturated fat) and ice cream.

Bibliography

Belle Boone Beard, 1967. *Social Competence of Centenarians.* Social Science Research Institute, University of Georgia, Athens, Georgia.

Robert N. Butler, 1975. *Why Survive?* Harper and Row, Publishers, New York.

Simone de Beauvoir, 1972. *Old Age.* G. P. Putnam's Sons, New York.

H. A. De Vries, 1968. *Report on Jogging and Exercise for Older Adults.* U.S. Administration on Aging, H. E. W., Washington, D.C.

A. L. Finkle *et al.*, 1959. *Journal of the American Medical Association* 170; 1391–3. (Potency among a sample of men aged between fifty-six and eighty-six.)

H. C. Lehman, 1953. *Age and Achievement.* Princeton University Press, Princeton, New Jersey.

H. Levinson, 1969. *Harvard Business Review* 47; (4) 51–60. (Middle-life reassessment.)

National Council on Aging, 1975. *The Myth and Reality of Aging in America.*

B. L. Neugarten, 1974. "Age Groups in American Society and the Rise of the Young-Old." *Annual of the New York Academy*; 187–198.

G. Newman and C. R. Nichols, 1960. *Journal of the American Medical Association* 173; 33–5. (Sexual activity of men and women between the ages of sixty and ninety-three.)

C. Patel and W. R. S. North, 1975. *Lancet* ii, 93. (Experiments with yoga-type relaxation and biofeedback to lower blood pressure.)

Raymond Pearl, 1930. *The Biology of Population Growth.* A. A. Knopf, Inc., New York.

E. Pfeiffer, A. Verwoerdt and H. S. Wang, 1968. *Archives of General Psychiatry* 19; 753–8. (The age range and frequency of sexual intercourse of men and women.)

Jackson K. Putman, 1970. *Old-Age Politics in California.* Stanford University Press, Stanford, California.

H. Zuckerman and R. K. Merton, 1972. *Aging and Society*, edited by M. W. Riley. Russell Sage, New York.

Index

Acknowledgements

The publishers gratefully acknowledge permission given by the following publishers and agents to reproduce copyright material: Barrie and Jenkins Ltd., London, and the University of Michigan Press for a quotation from *Dialogues in Limbo* by George Santayana. Curtis Brown Ltd., on behalf of the Executors of the Estate of Lin Yutang. André Deutsch Ltd., for a quotation from *Conversations with Kafka* by Gustav Janouch. The *Observer* newspaper for quotations by Bernard Baruch in *Sayings of the Week,* 21st August 1955, and Pablo Picasso in *Shouts and Murmurs,* reprinted from *Picasso in Private* by John Richardson. Laurence Pollinger Ltd., on behalf of the Helena Rubinstein Estate. A. P. Watt and Son on behalf of the Executors of the Estate of W. Somerset Maugham.

The following have granted permission for reproduction of their photographs in this volume: Bavaria Verlag pp. 17, 33; Camera Press pp. 23, 28; Colorific p. 27 right; Robert Harding Associates p. 10 centre; Alan Hutchison p. 10 left; PAF International pp. 9, 14–15, 16, 21 right, 23 left, 29, 30–31; Pictorial Press p. 25; Picturepoint pp. 12, 13, 18, 19, 21 left, 26, 32; Rex Features p. 20; ZEFA (UK) p. 24. In addition, the following have provided material for use as artist's reference: Associated Press; Eric Auerbach; Professor Belle Boone Beard, Sweet Briar College, Virginia; Black Star (Ralph Crane); Camera Press; The China Photo Service; Colorific; Zoe Dominic; The Mary Evans Picture Library; Hope Enterprises; Keystone Press; *The Los Angeles Times;* Mansell Collection; Jean Mermet; Norsk Folkemuseum, Oslo; Novosti; Penguin Books; Pictorial Parade; Pictorial Press; Popperfoto; Radio Times Hulton Picture Library; Rex Features; Collection Sirot, Paris; Syndication International.